3-

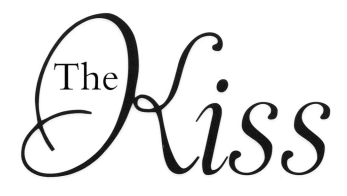

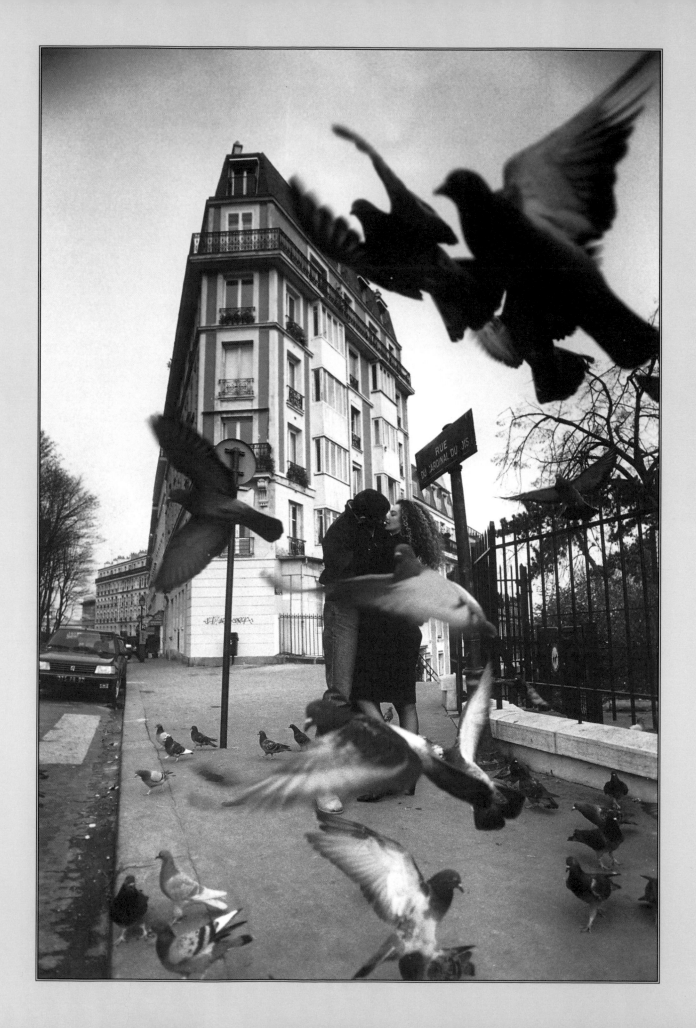

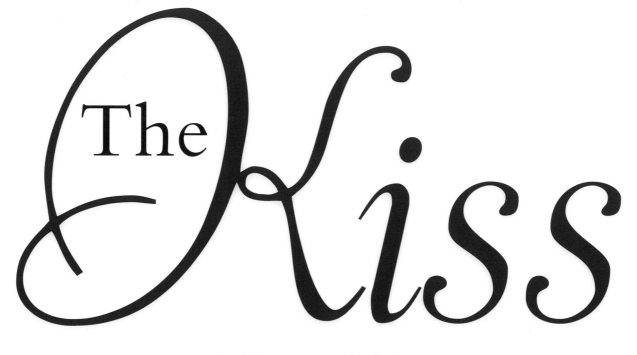

The Kiss

A Romantic Treasury

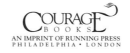

COURAGE BOOKS
AN IMPRINT OF RUNNING PRESS
PHILADELPHIA · LONDON

9 8 7 6 5 4 3 2 1
Digit on the right indicates the number of this printing

Library of Congress Cataloging-in-Publication Number 00-131793

ISBN 0-7624-0877-4

Cover and interior design by MaryAnn Katowitz
and Frances J. Soo Ping Chow
Edited by Molly Jay
Typography: Bembo, Futura, and Viant

This book may be ordered by mail from the publisher.
But try your bookstore first!

Published by Courage Books, an imprint of
Running Press Book Publishers
125 South Twenty-second Street
Philadelphia, Pennsylvania 19103-4399

Visit us on the web!
www.runningpress.com

Contents

Introduction

The heart can discern so many kinds of kisses: from the pivotal first peck to the hungry, warm urgency that punctuates a tryst. A kiss is a singular bond, a crystallized moment that embodies the relationship of the kisser to the kissed. In a world where words are easily misconstrued, kisses are eloquent.

Soft and reassuring as butterscotch, a kiss nourishes and worms the soul. It is a confection that never grows tiresome. And when it is over, it lingers on the lips and lives in memory.

Talking about kissing is like humming about fire. Words are insufficient to describe the experience. Still we try, because kissing is an experience that must be shared.

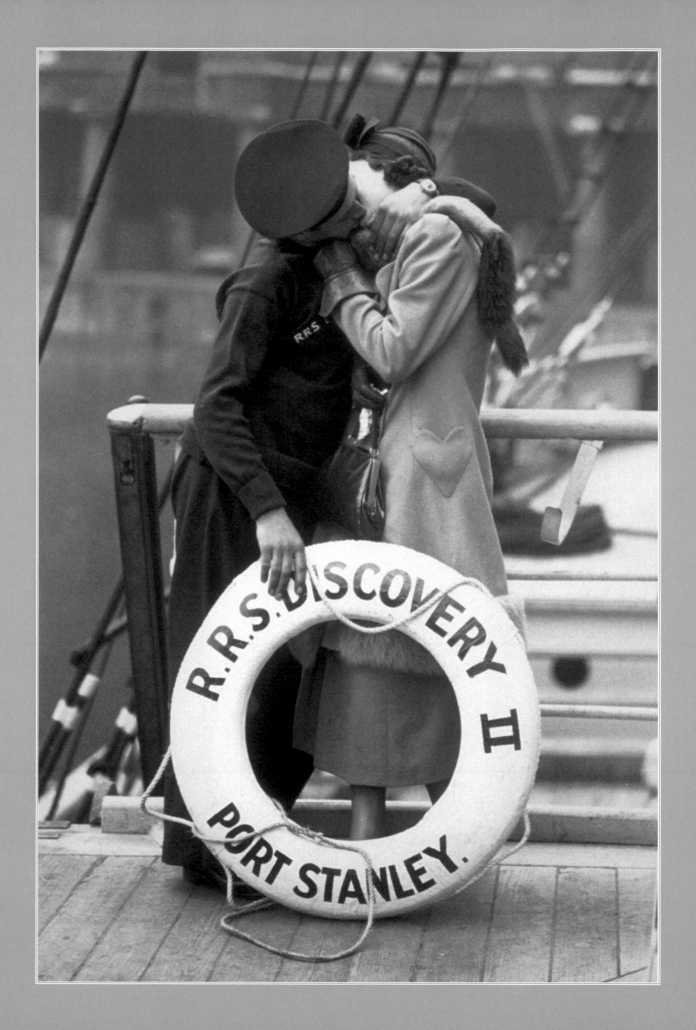

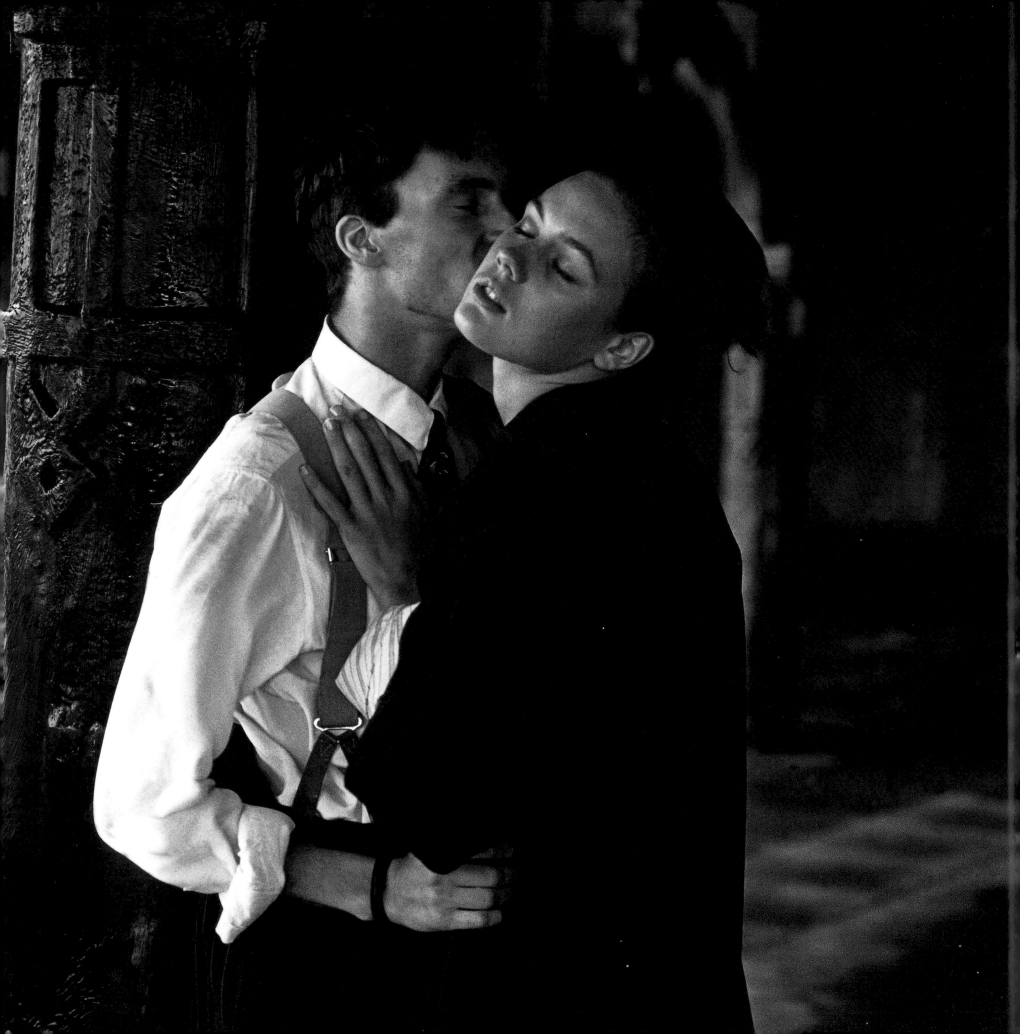

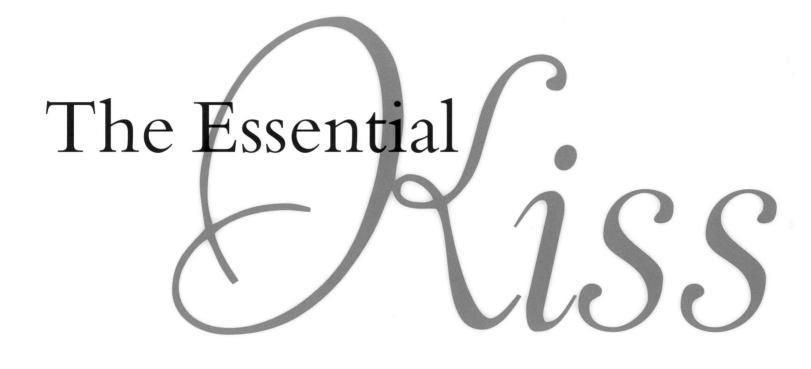

*S*oul meets soul on lovers lips.

Percy Bysshe Shelly (1792-1822)
English Poet

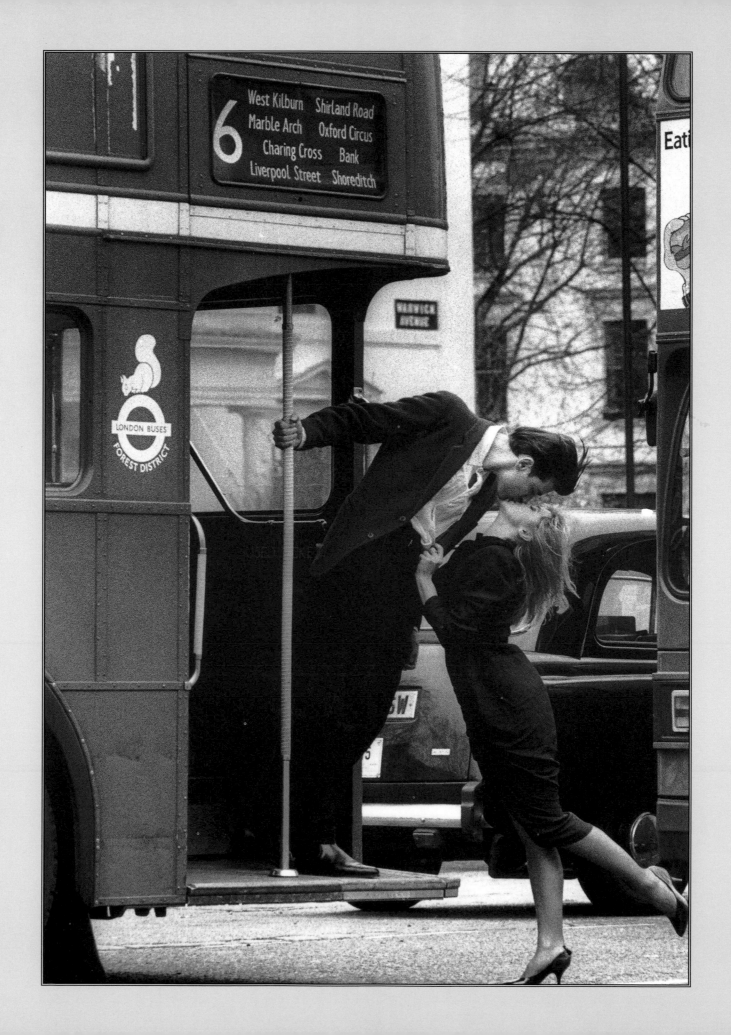

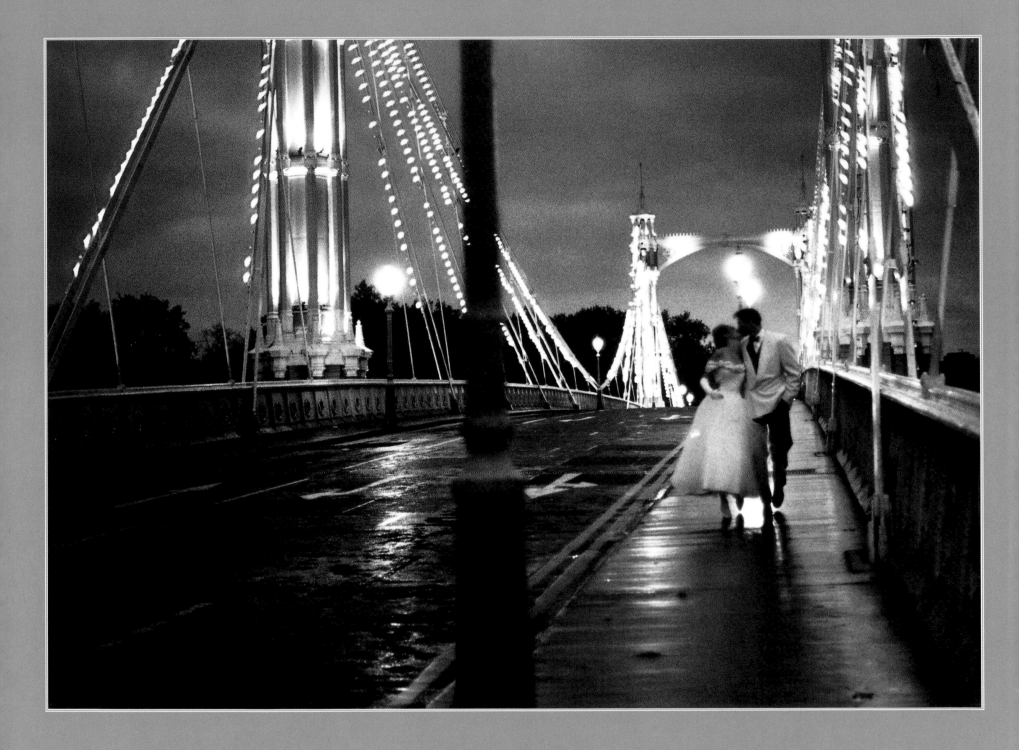

they loved dearly; their souls kissed, they kissed with their eyes,
they were both but one single kiss!

Heinrich Heine (1797-1856)
German poet

. . . once he drew
With one long kiss my whole soul thro
My lips, as sunlight drinketh dew.

Alfred, Lord Tennyson (1809-1892)
English poet

What of soul was left,
I wonder, when the kissing
had to stop?

Robert Browning (1812-1889)
English Poet

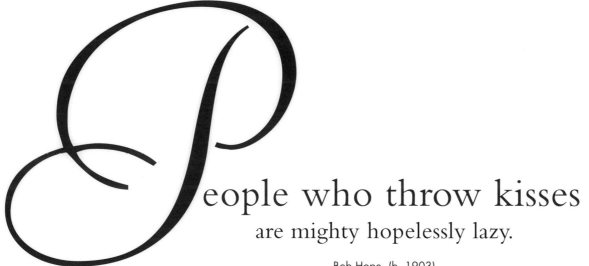

People who throw kisses
are mighty hopelessly lazy.

Bob Hope, (b. 1903)
American Comedian

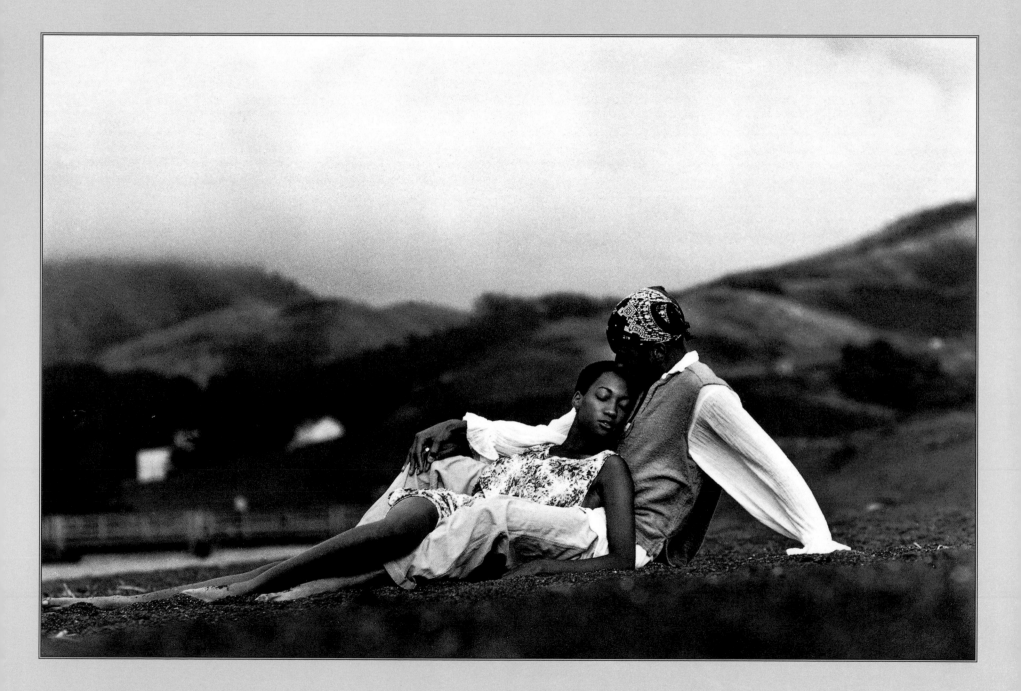

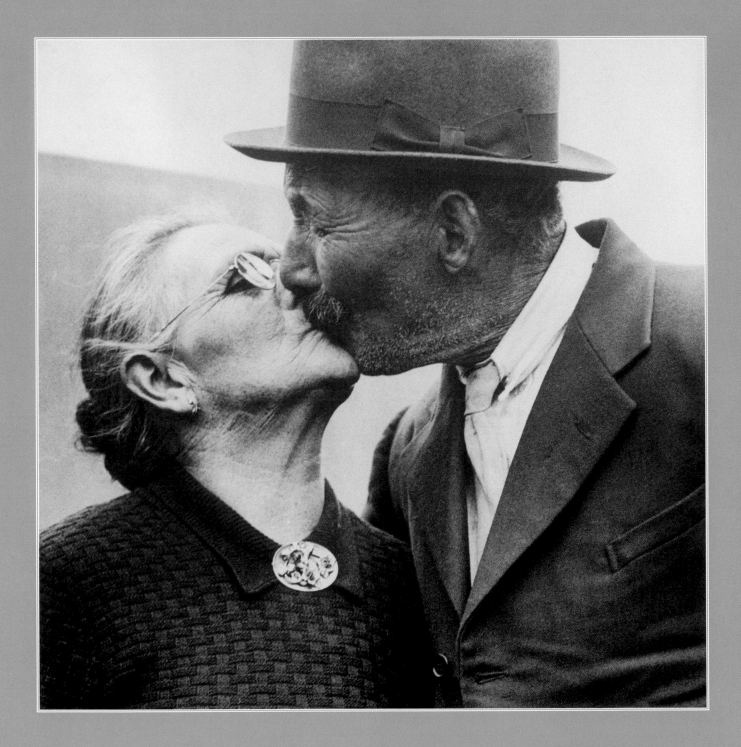

Kisses

are like grains of gold or silver found upon the ground, of no value themselves,

but precious as showing that a mine is near.

George Villiers (1628-1687)
English courtier and dramatist

There is the kiss of welcome and of parting; the long, lingering, loving, present one; the stolen, or the mutual one; the kiss of love, of joy, and of sorrow; the seal of promise and receipt of fulfillment.

Thomas C. Haliburton (1796-1865)
Canadian humorist and jurist

A kiss is something you cannot give without taking and cannot take without giving.

Anonymous

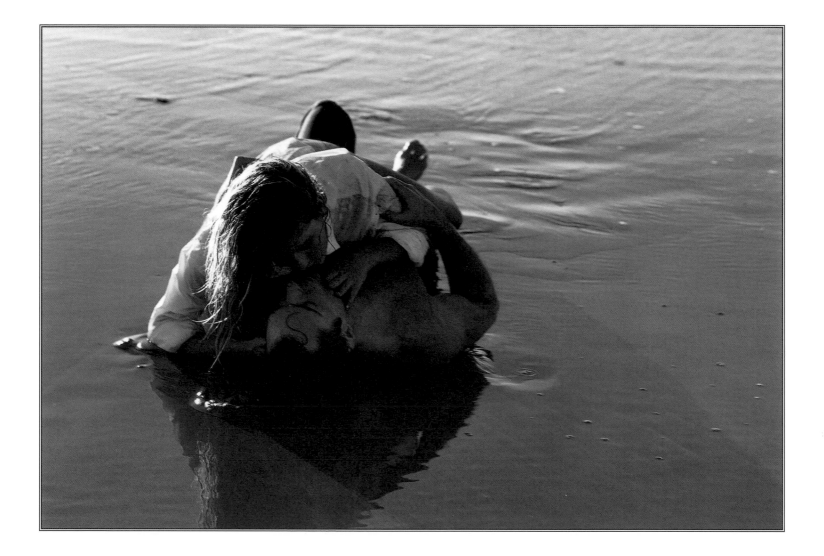

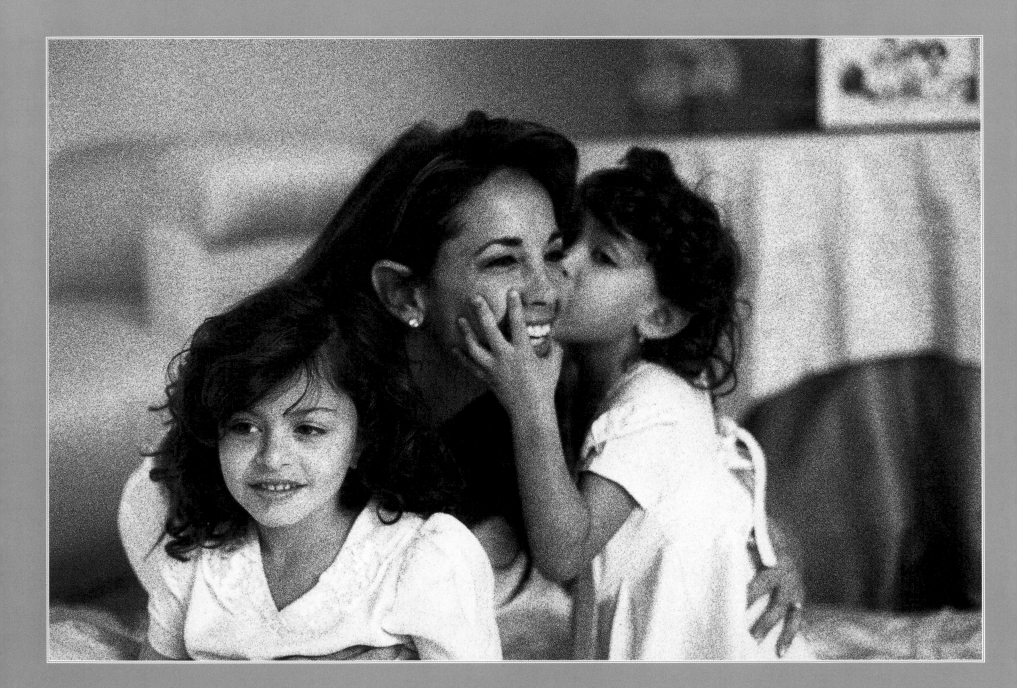

A kiss is the shortest distance
between two.

Henny Youngman (1906-1998)
English-born American comedian

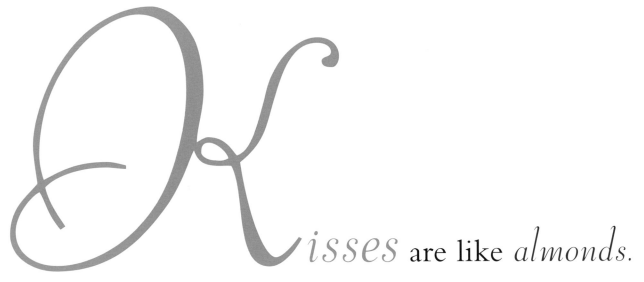

*K*isses are like *almonds.*

Maltese Proverb

. . . *kisses* are a better fate than wisdom.

e.e. cummings (1894-1962)
American poet

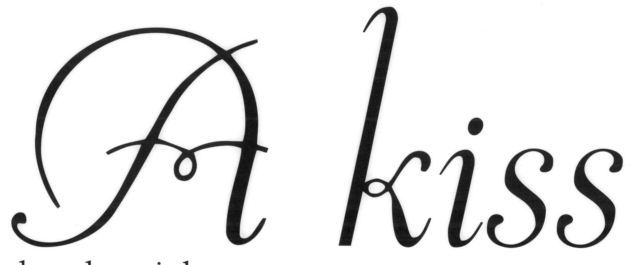

is a lovely trick designed by nature to stop speech
when words become superfluous.

Ingrid Bergman (1915-1982)
Swedish actress

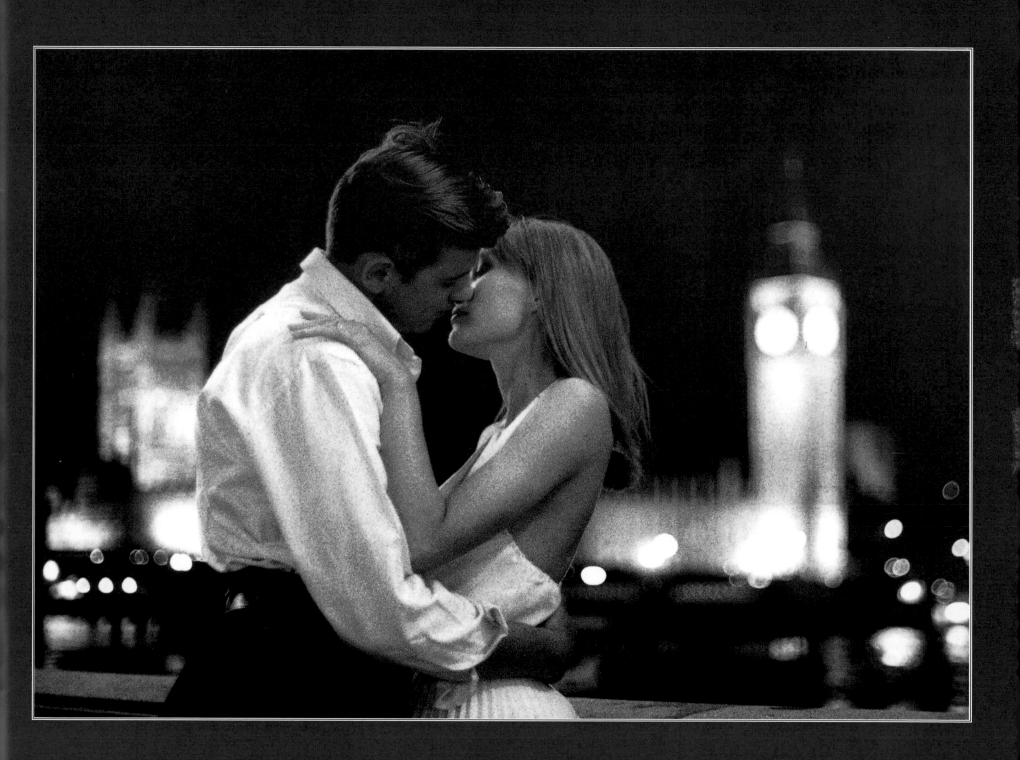

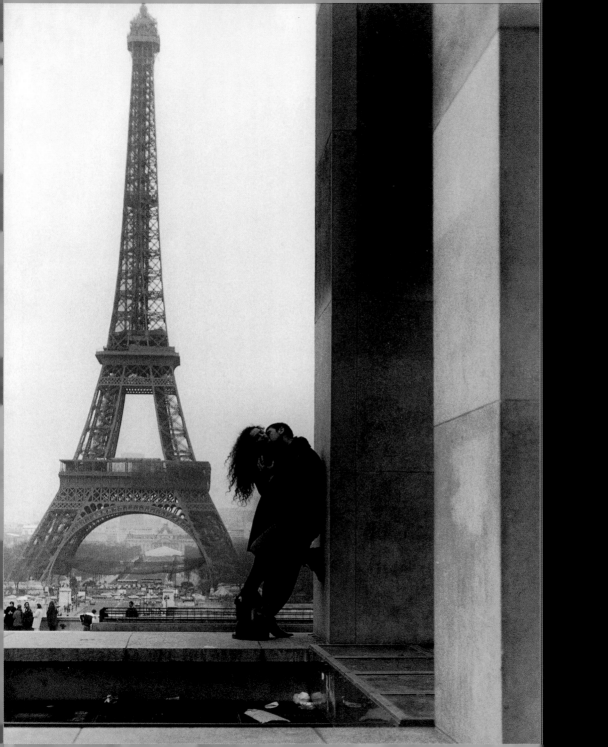

A kiss is
the anatomical juxtaposition
of two orbicular muscles in a state of contraction.

Cary Grant (1904-1986)
[quoting Dr. Henry Gibbons]
English-born American actor

Her lips on his could tell him better
than all her stumbling words.

Margaret Mitchell (1900-1949)
American writer

We embraced each other with—how to say it?—a momentous smiling calm, as if the cup of language had silently overflowed into these eloquent kisses which replaced words like the rewards of silence itself, perfecting thought and gesture.

Lawrence Durrell (1912-1990)
English writer

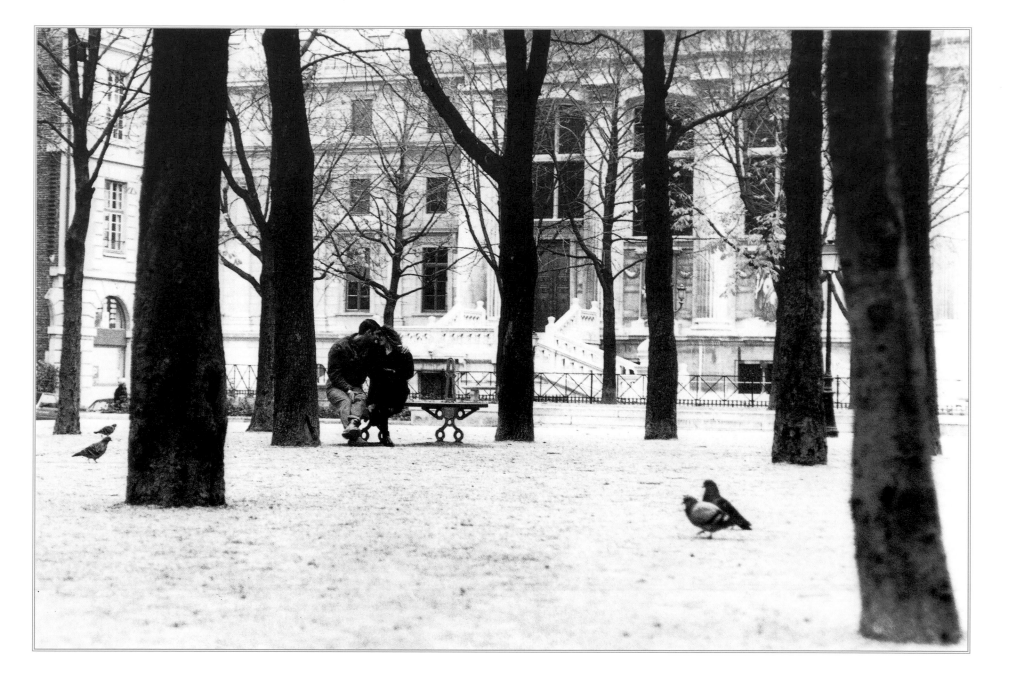

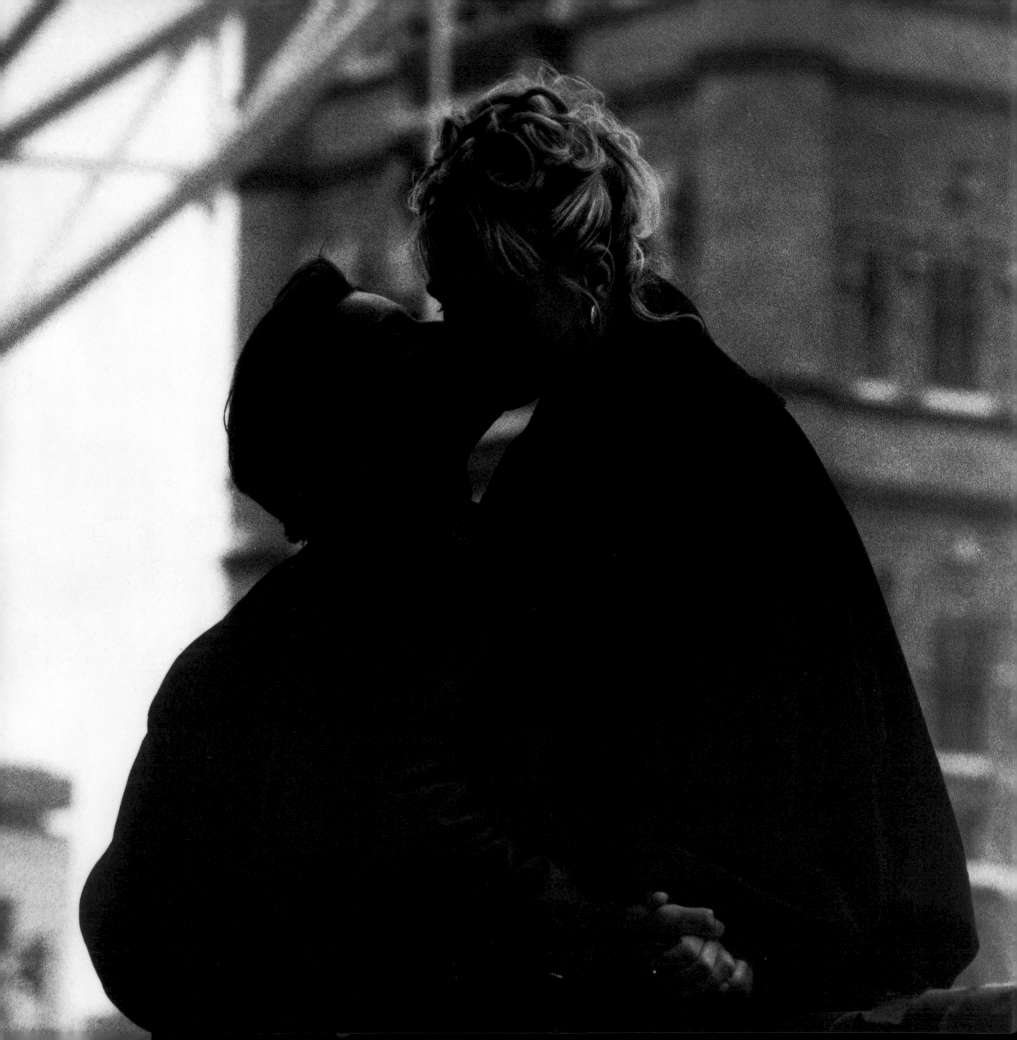

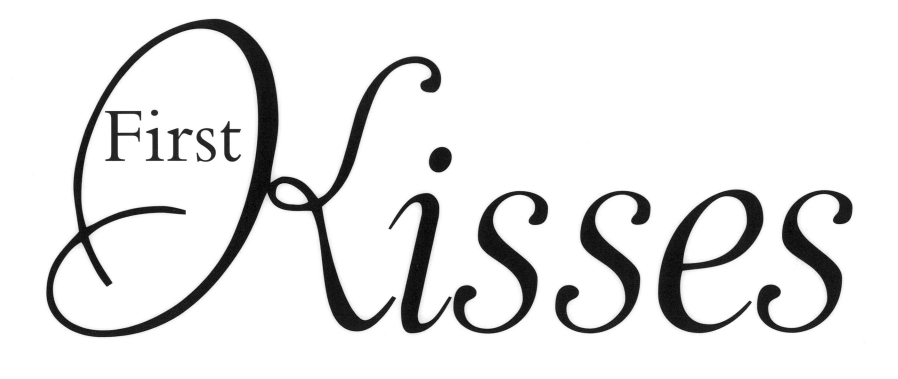

Lord! I wonder what fool it was that first invented kissing.

Jonathan Swift (1667-1745)
English satirist

The kiss originated when the first male reptile licked the first female reptile, implying in a subtle, complimentary way that she was as succulent as the small reptile he had for dinner the night before.

F. Scott Fitzgerald (1880-1956)
American writer

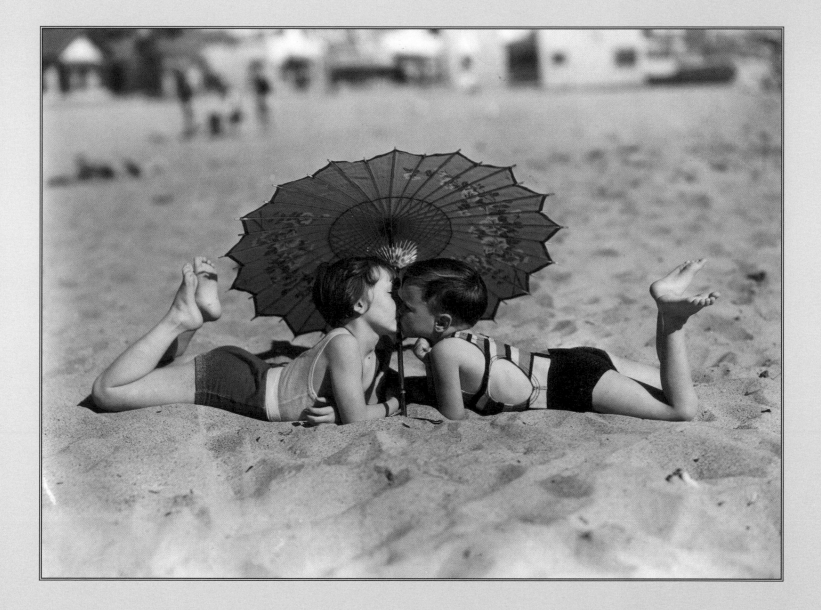

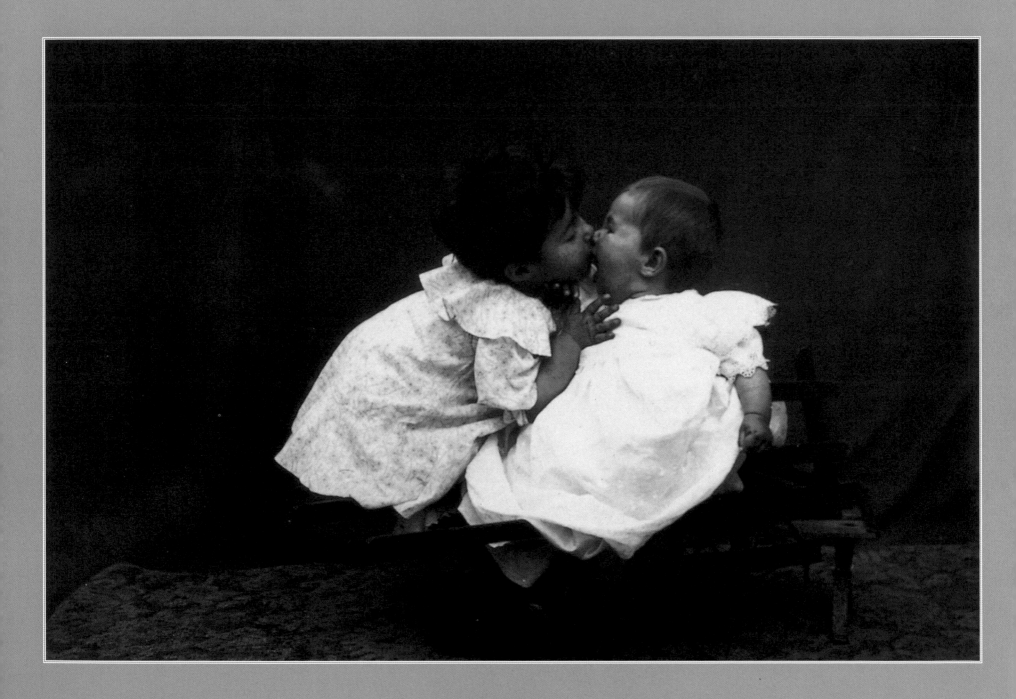

The decision to kiss *for the first time* is the most crucial in any love story. *It* changes the relationship *of two people* much more strongly than even the final surrender; *because this kiss already has within it that surrender.*

Emil Ludwig (1881-1948)
German biographer

"I don't know how to kiss, or I would kiss you.

Where do the noses go?"

Dudley Nichols
Author of the screenplay *For Whom The Bell Tolls,*
based on the novel by Ernest Hemingway

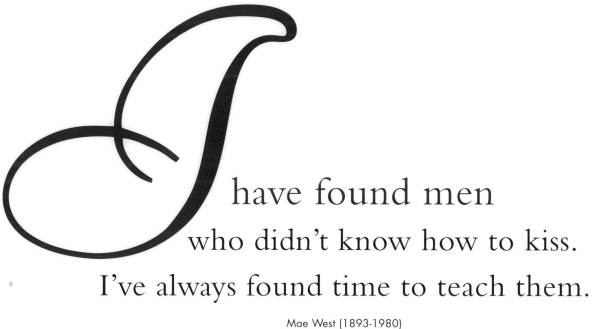 have found men
who didn't know how to kiss.
I've always found time to teach them.

Mae West (1893-1980)
American actress

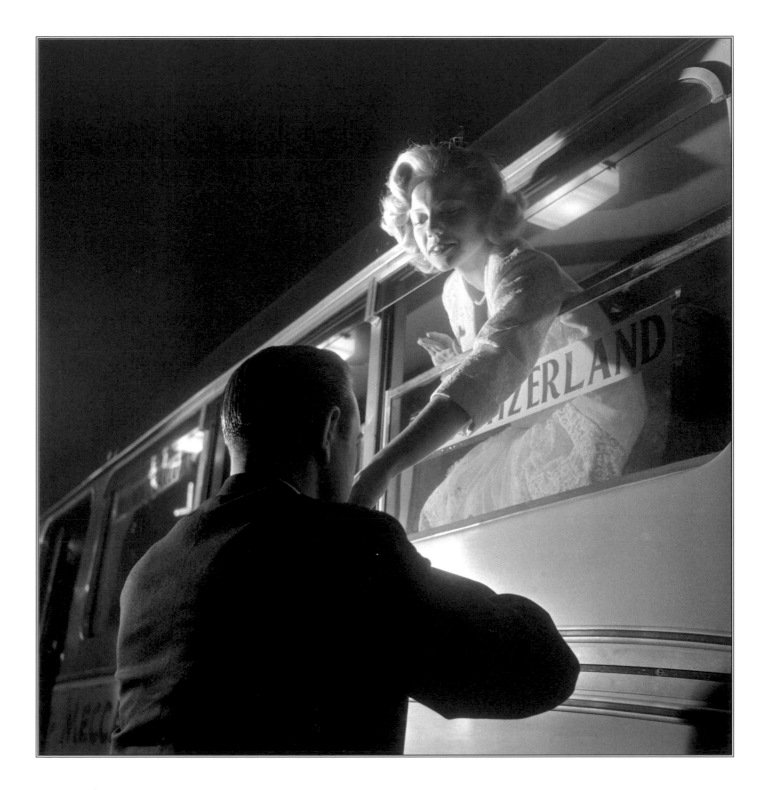

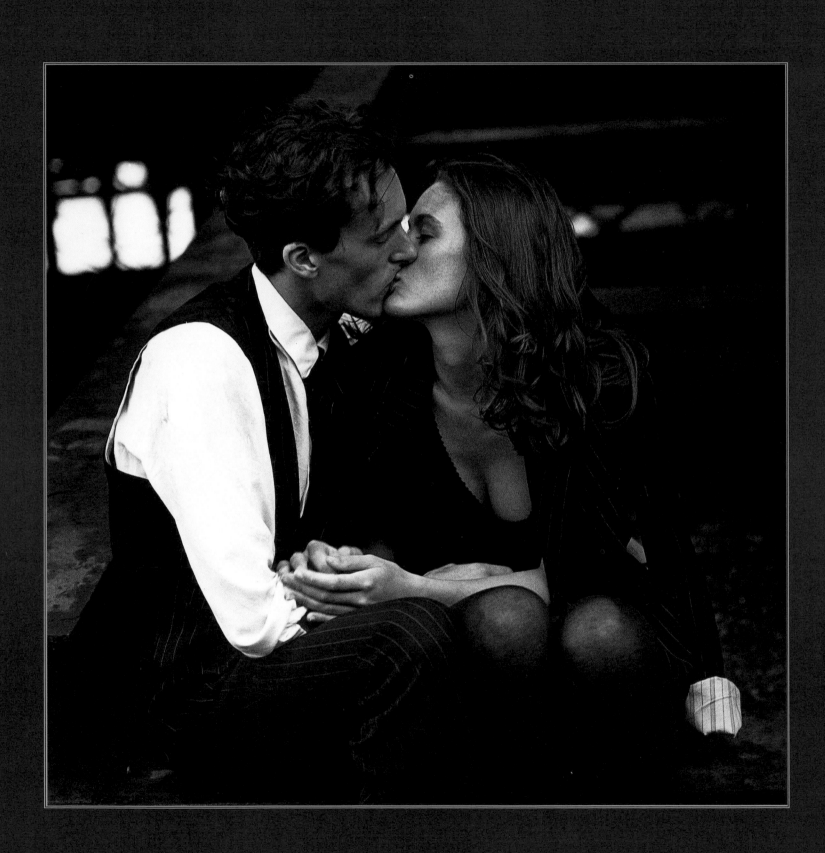

"Scarlett, you need kissing badly. That's what's wrong with you. . . . You should be kissed and by someone who knows how."

"And I suppose you think you are the proper person?" she asked. . . .

"Oh, yes, if I cared to take the trouble," he said carelessly. "They say I kiss very well . . . take heart. Some day I will kiss you and you will like it. But not now, so I beg you not to be too impatient."

Gone With The Wind
Margaret Mitchell (1900-1949)
American writer

Give me a kiss,
and to that kiss a score;

Then to that twenty,
add a hundred more:

A thousand to that hundred:
so kiss on,

To make that thousand
up a million.

Treble that million,
and when that is done,

Let's kiss afresh,
as when we first begun.

Robert Herrick (1591-1674)
English poet

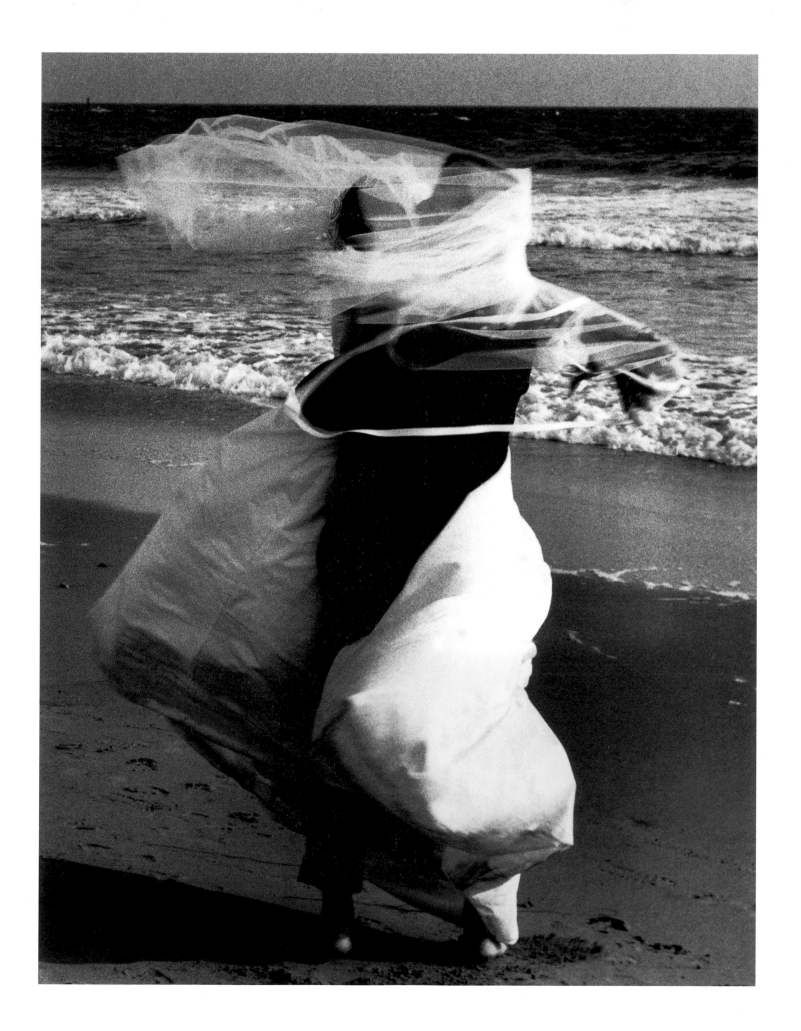

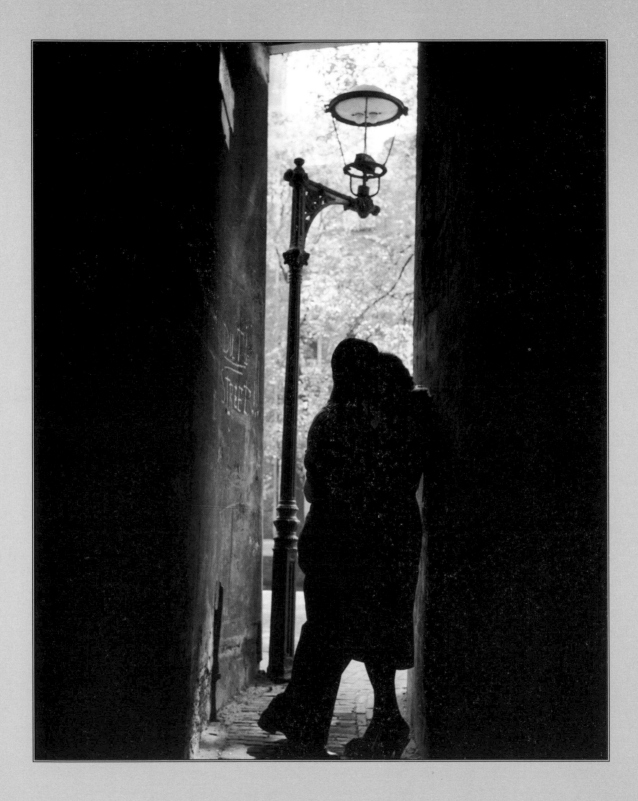

Their kiss

was accompanied by the street organ and it lasted the whole length of the musical score of Carmen, and when it ended **it was too late;** they had drunk the potion to its last drop. Then potion drunk by lovers is prepared by no one but themselves.

Anaïs Nin (1903-1977)
French-born American writer

In delay there lies no plenty;
Then come kiss me, sweet and twenty,
Youth's a stuff will not endure."

William Shakespeare (1564-1616)
English dramatist and poet

That first night . . . she kissed me.
My lips felt so hot, I thought they would burst into flames.
She held me and wanted to do more, but I was too frightened,
just a fumbling schoolboy of fourteen.

Kirk Douglas (b.1916)
American actor

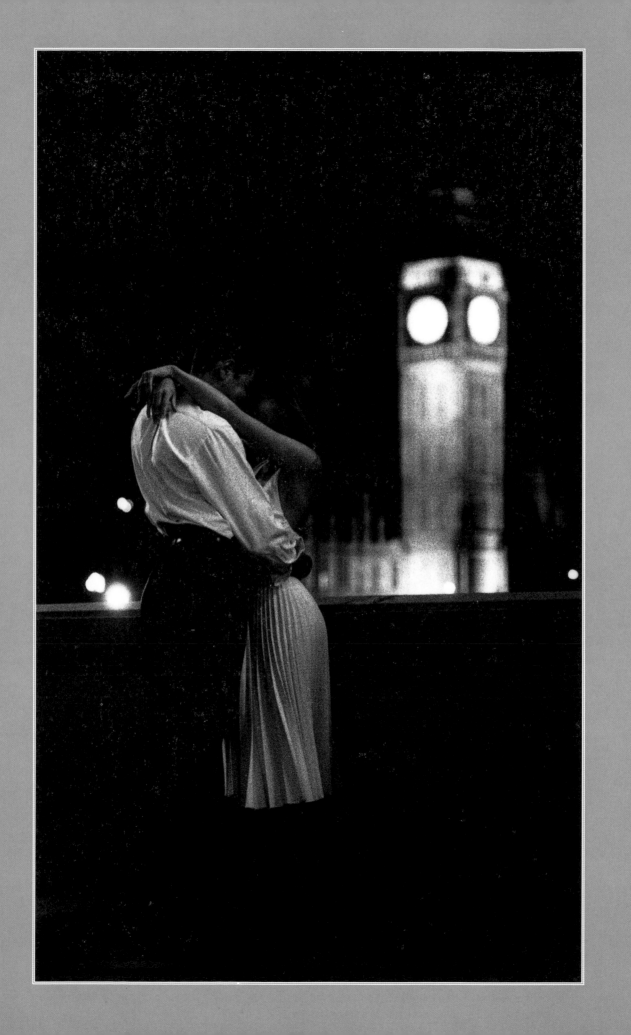

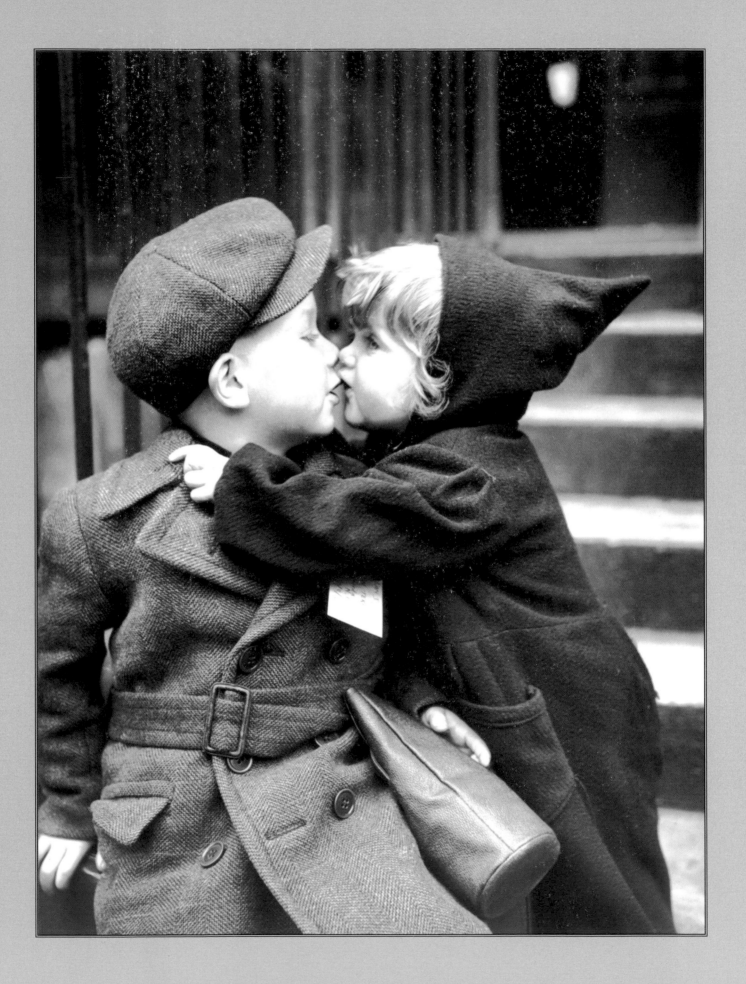

. . . *My* "first" kiss . . .

I actually asked her permission. She sighed, as in resignation,

and then with some impatience she closed her eyes, puckered her lips and then

opened them only long enough to say, "Okay but make it quick," whereupon

we engaged in the briefest and driest moment in all erotica.

Phil Donahue (b. 1935)
American talk-show host

We hadn't been able to see from our position whether the kiss had actually happened, but when Frankie told us it was safe to come out, he swore it had.

"What's it like?" I asked.

"It tastes like chewing gum," Frankie replied.

Russell Baker (b.1924)
American journalist

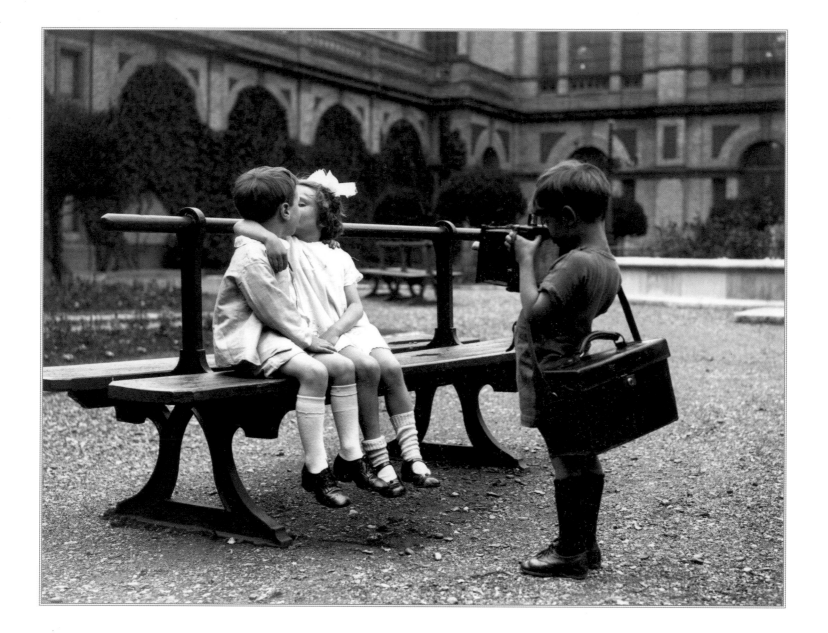

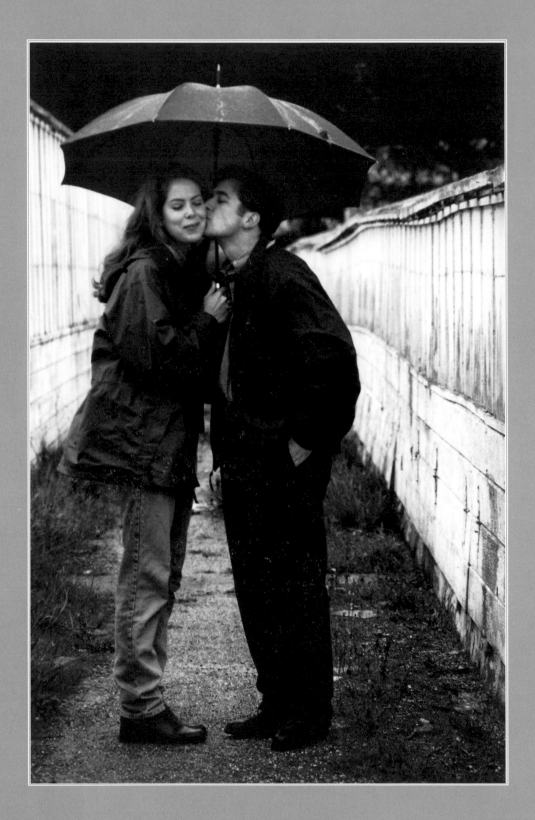

The kissing game I most vividly remember was called Seven Minutes in Heaven. The two players went into the closet where they were supposed to find celestial bliss by spending seven minutes kissing. Of course, there was no . . . clock in the closet: just a boy and girl who wondered why they were feeling less passion than fear . . .

Bill Cosby (b. 1937)
American actor

I think *he is going to kiss me.*
I wonder how I will breathe. I remember . . . it's much better
not to think things through too much, just to do them. So I do. . . .
He kisses me. . . . His closeness must have an antihistamine effect,
because, though we kiss for a long time, I am able to breathe.

Ellyn Bache
20th century American writer

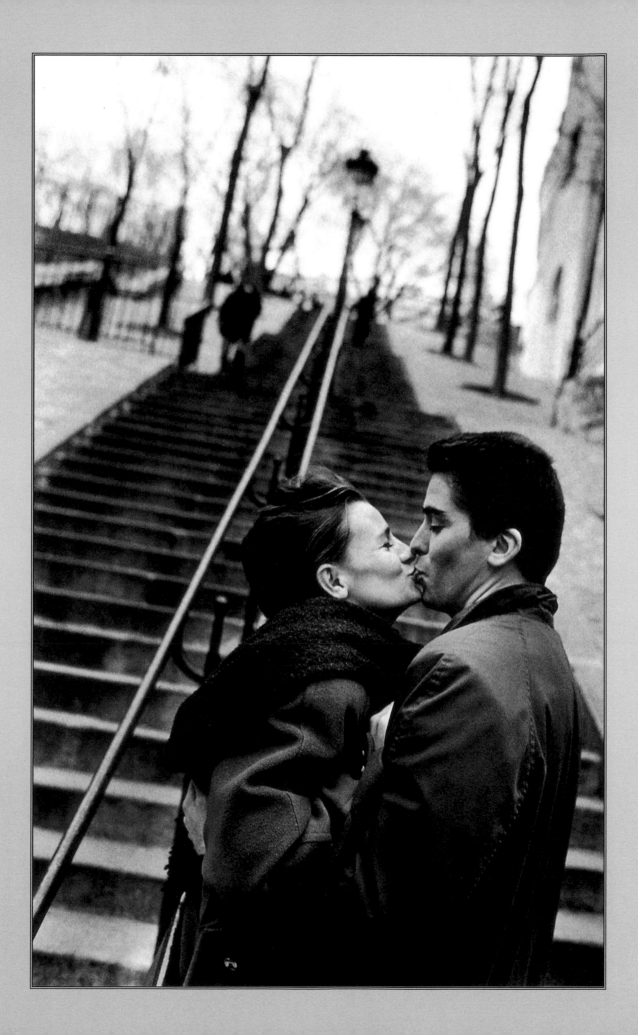

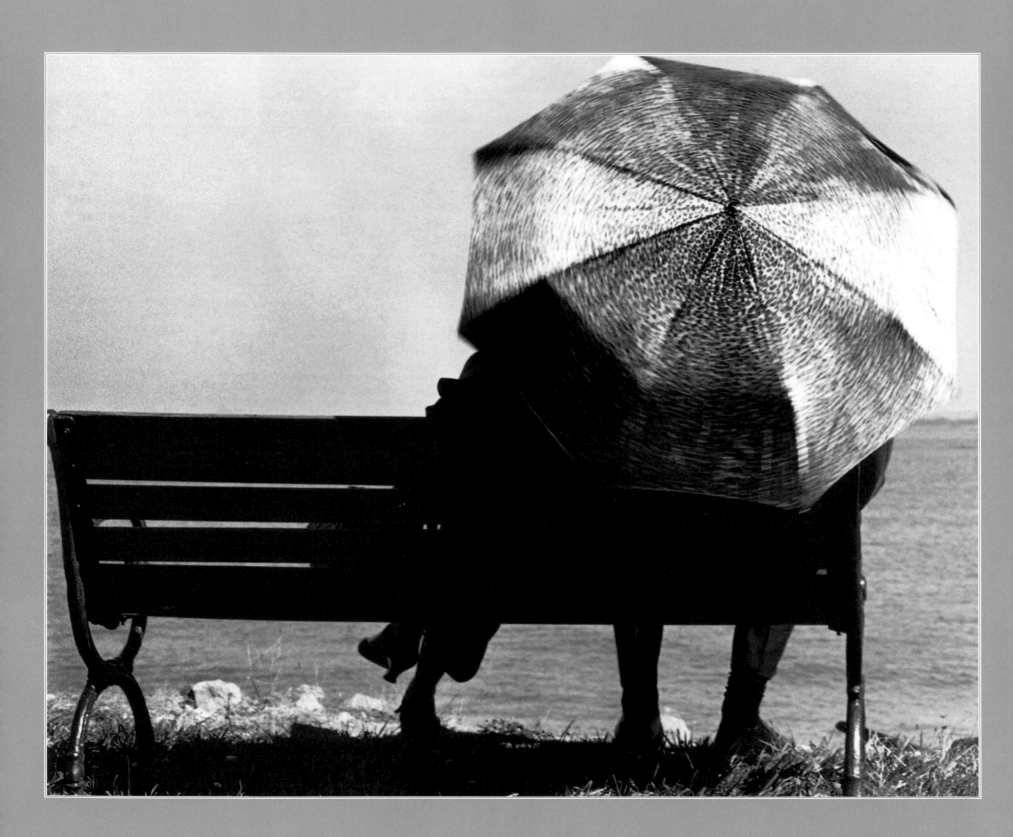

Women still remember the first kiss
after men have forgotten the last.

Remy de Gourmont (1858-1915)
French novelist and philosopher

A recent study shows that, among men,

99 percent report that their first kiss was exciting;

among women, only 76 percent found their first kiss exciting.

Louis Rukeyser (b. 1933)
American financial broadcaster

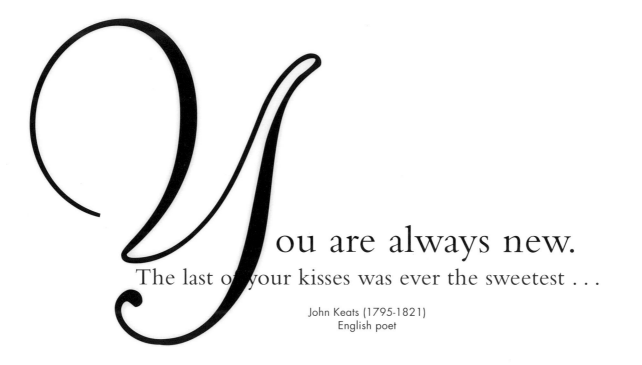

You are always new.
The last of your kisses was ever the sweetest . . .

John Keats (1795-1821)
English poet

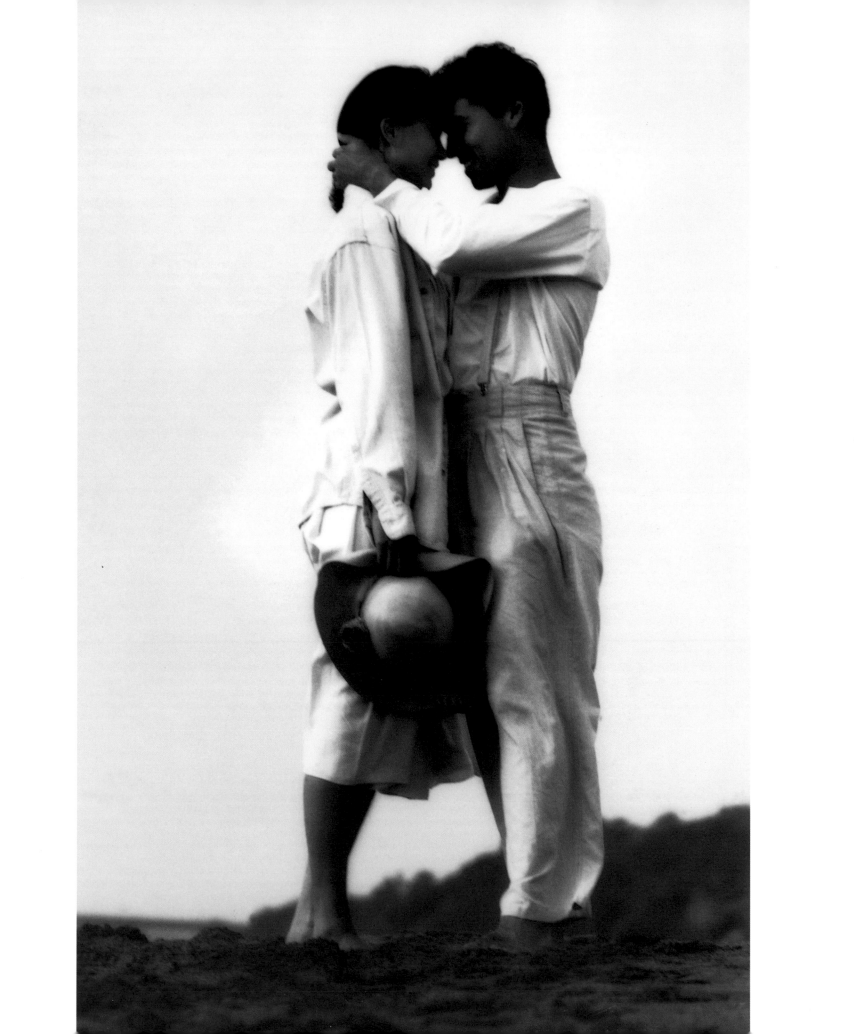

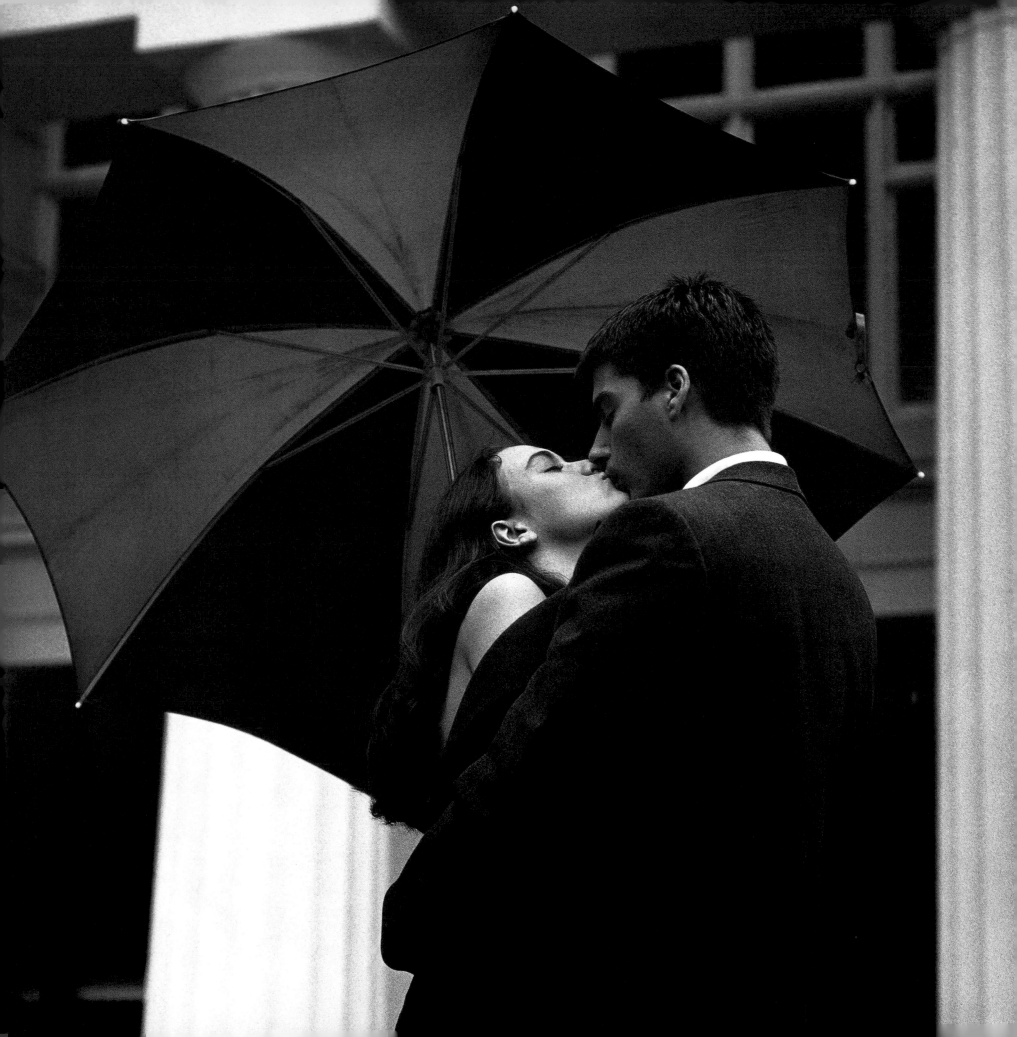

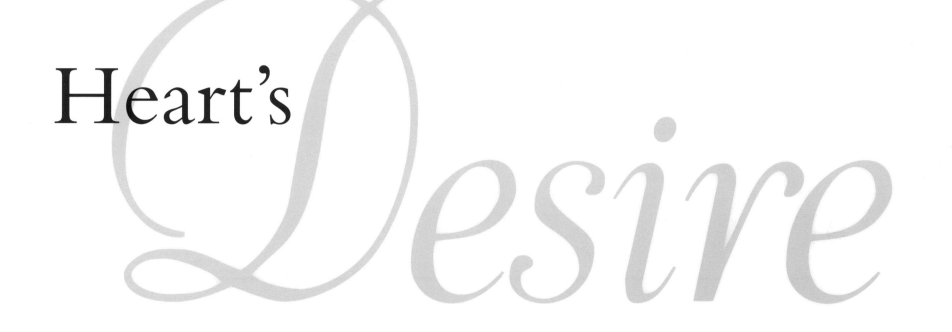

Heart's *Desire*

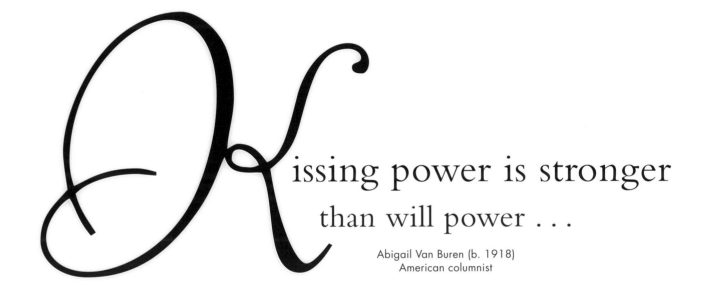

Kissing power is stronger
than will power . . .

Abigail Van Buren (b. 1918)
American columnist

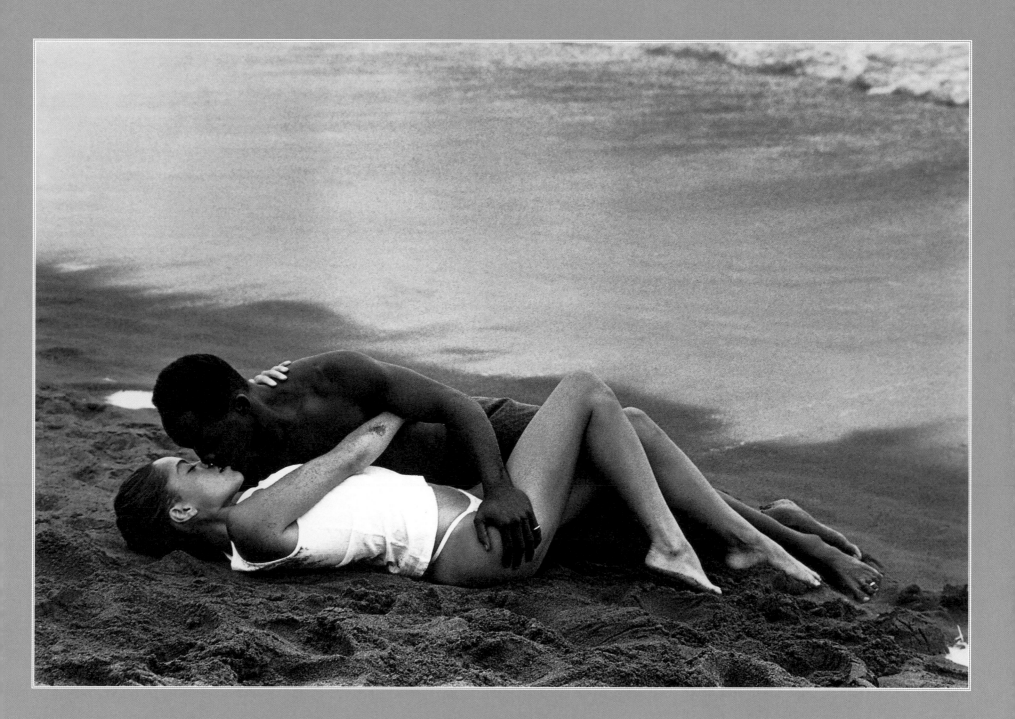

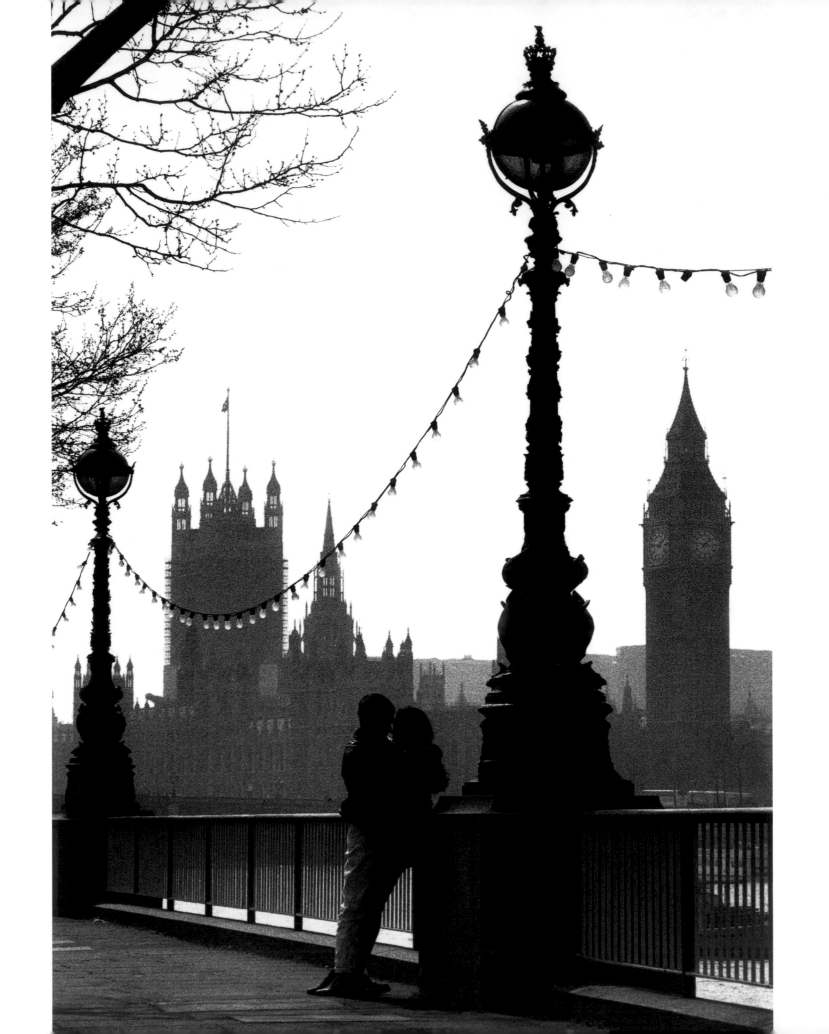

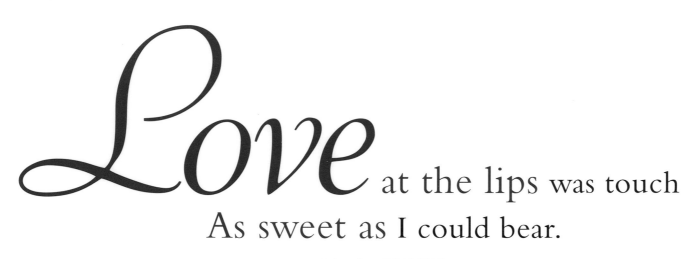

Love at the lips was touch
As sweet as I could bear.

Robert Frost (1874-1963)
American poet

The moment eternal—
just that and no more—
When ecstasy's utmost
        we clutch at the core,
While cheeks burn,
arms open, eyes shut,
and lips meet!

Robert Browning (1812-1889)
English poet

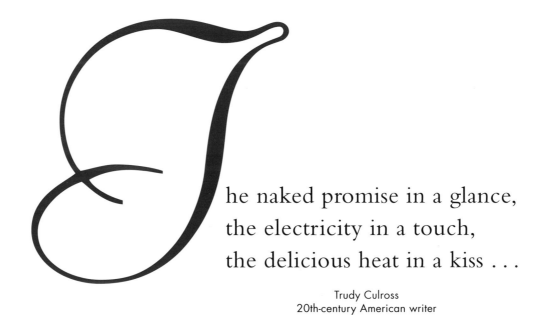

The naked promise in a glance,
the electricity in a touch,
the delicious heat in a kiss . . .

Trudy Culross
20th-century American writer

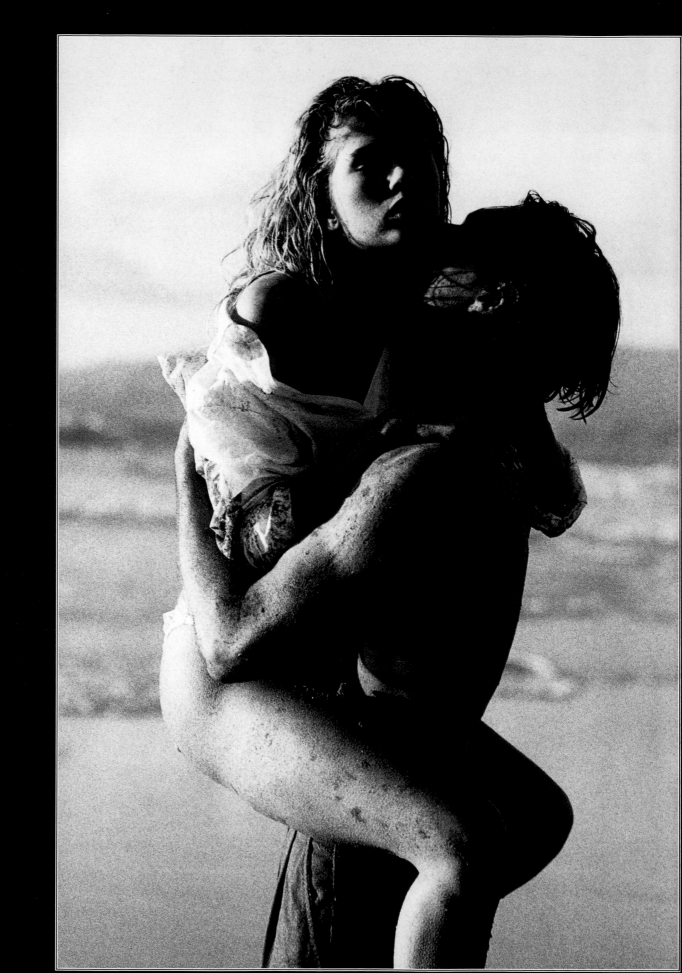

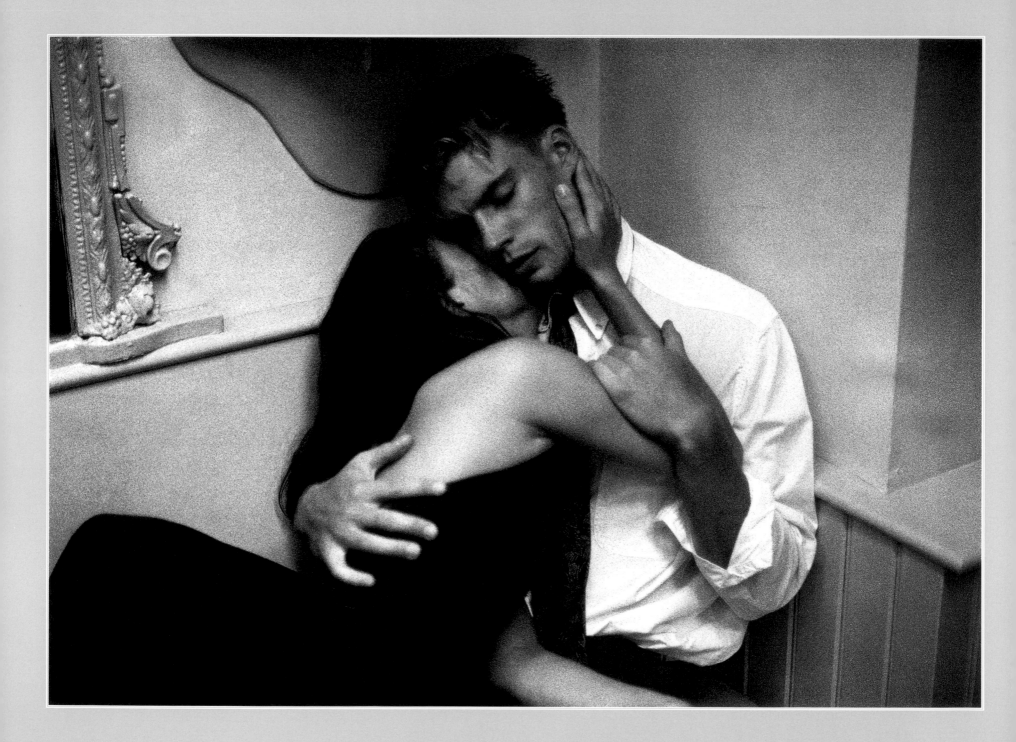

When we reached the place for goodnight
I could not let him go as he had always done before,
but put my hands round his head and drew it down to mine
and kissed his mouth and looked close into
his eyes. And . . . he caught me in his arms and
pressed me to him and kissed my mouth and my eyes and my neck;
blindly and fiercely he kissed me. . . .
When I was in bed I could not sleep, but lay trembling
half with fear, half with wonder, at what
I had awakened in him.

Helen Thomas
19th-century English writer

. . . She bowed his head

and joined her lips to his. . . .
It was too much for him.
He closed his eyes,
surrendering himself to her,
body and mind,
conscious of nothing in the world
but the dark pressure
of her softly parting lips.

James Joyce (1882-1941)
Irish writer

*It was a strange sensation, a clumsy stumbling falling
being caught, the broad sunlit world narrowing to the dark focus
of his cushiony lips on mine. It scared me to death,
but still I discovered how much I had been waiting for it.*

Jane Smiley (b. 1949)
American writer

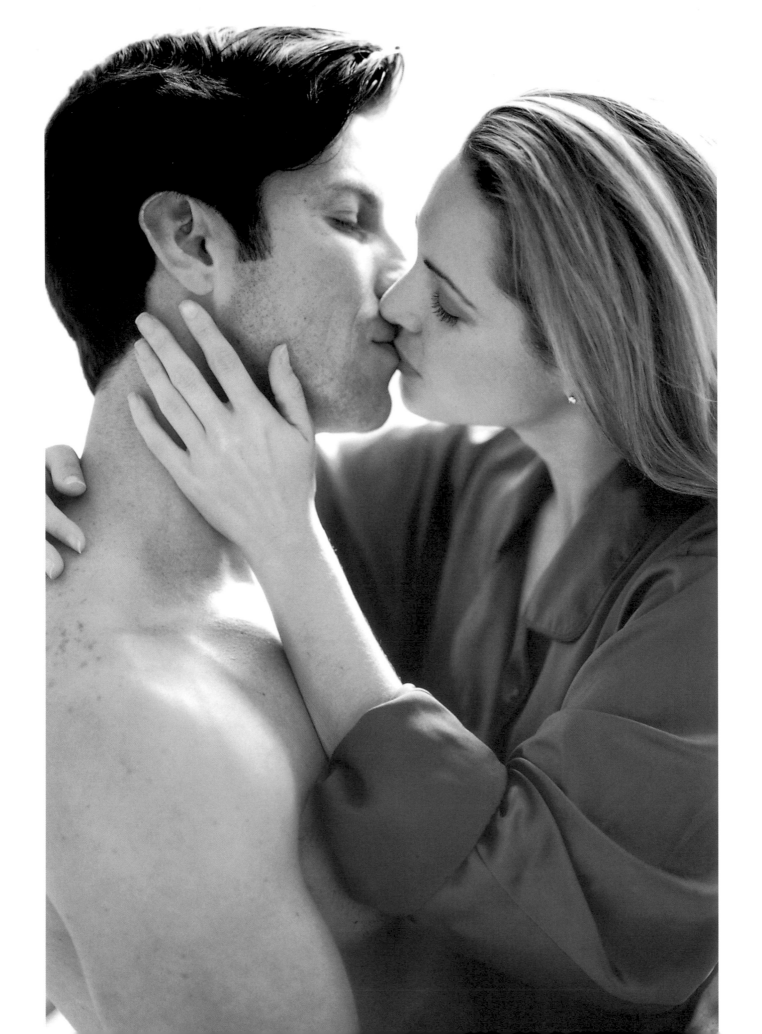

As we were sitting together, suddenly there came into her eyes a look that I had never seen there before. My lips moved towards hers.

We kissed each other.

I can't describe to you what I felt at that moment. It seemed to me that all my life had been narrowed to one perfect moment of rosecoloured joy.

Oscar Wilde (1854-1900)
British writer

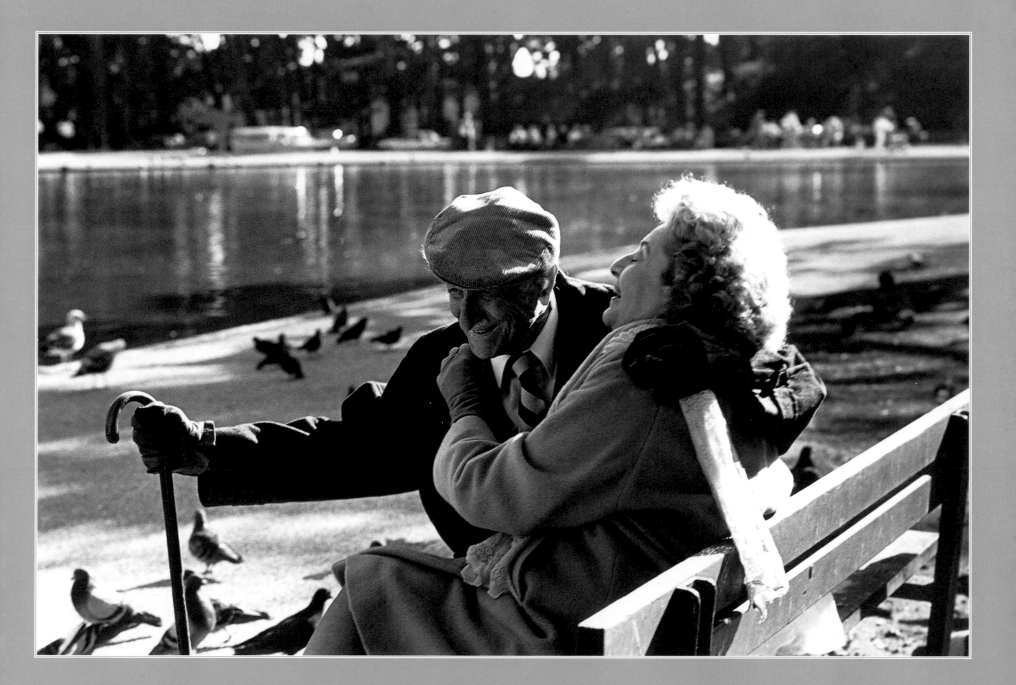

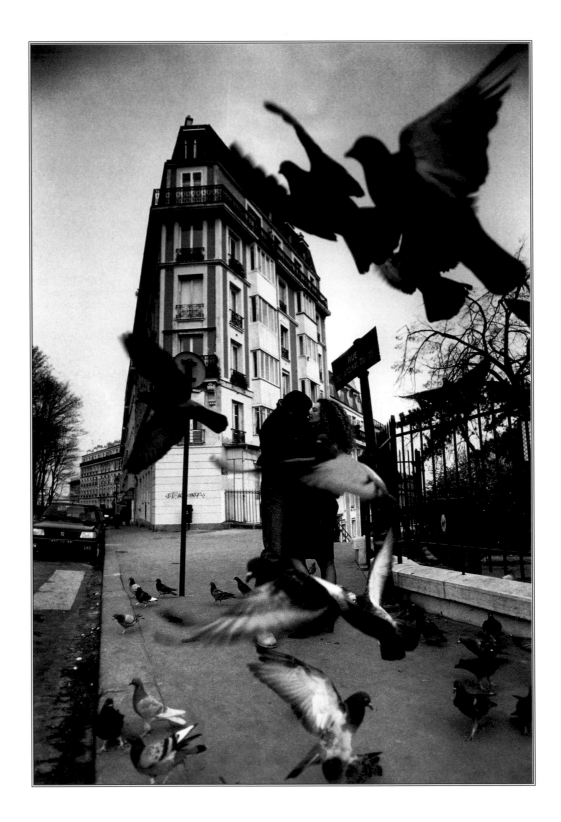

Was this the face that launched
a thousand ships
And burnt the topless towers of Ilium?
Sweet Helen, make me immortal
with a kiss!
Her lips suck forth my soul;
see where it flies!
Come Helen, give me my soul again.
Here I dwell, for Heaven is in these lips. . . .

Christopher Marlowe (1564-1593)
English dramatist

...she lifted her face *suddenly to him, and he touched it with his lips. So cold, so fresh, so sea-clear her face was, it was like kissing a flower that grows near the surf.*

D.H. Lawrence (1885-1930)
English writer

The kiss in the taxi . . . remains in the memory as perpetually unfinished and to be sought out again, for as the taxi moves it gives to the moment that physical proof of insecurity and ephemeralness of adventure, over swift, arousing resonances which cease at first stop. . . .

The adventure continues in the head, in the body. . . . Until the next taxi ride no kiss will have that flavor of life and time slipping by, uncapturable, unseizable.

Anaïs Nin (1903-1977)
French-born American writer

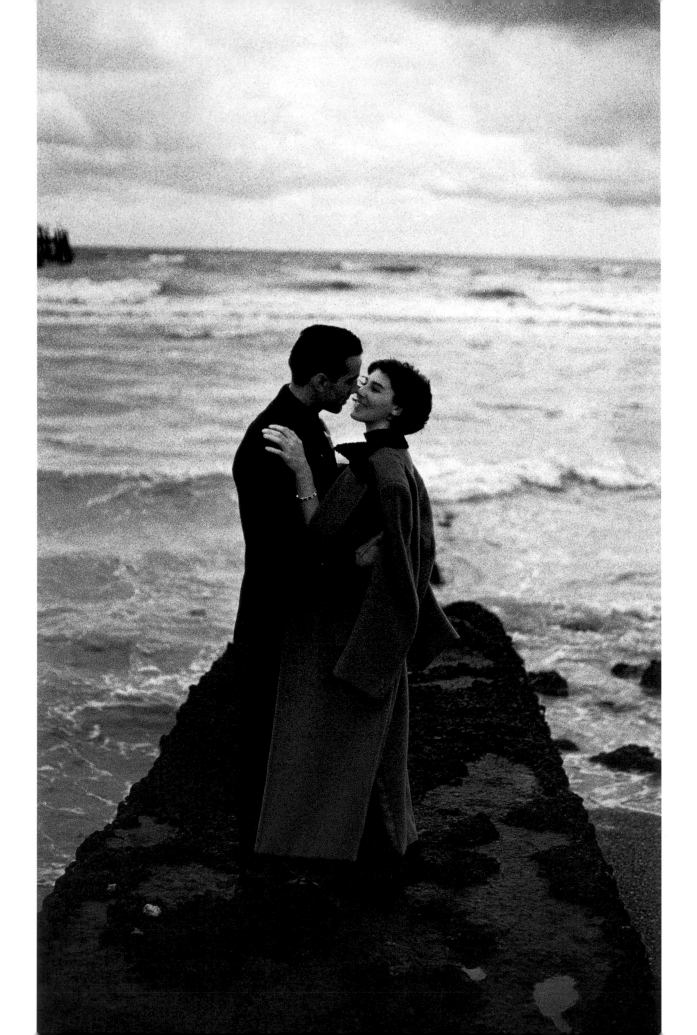

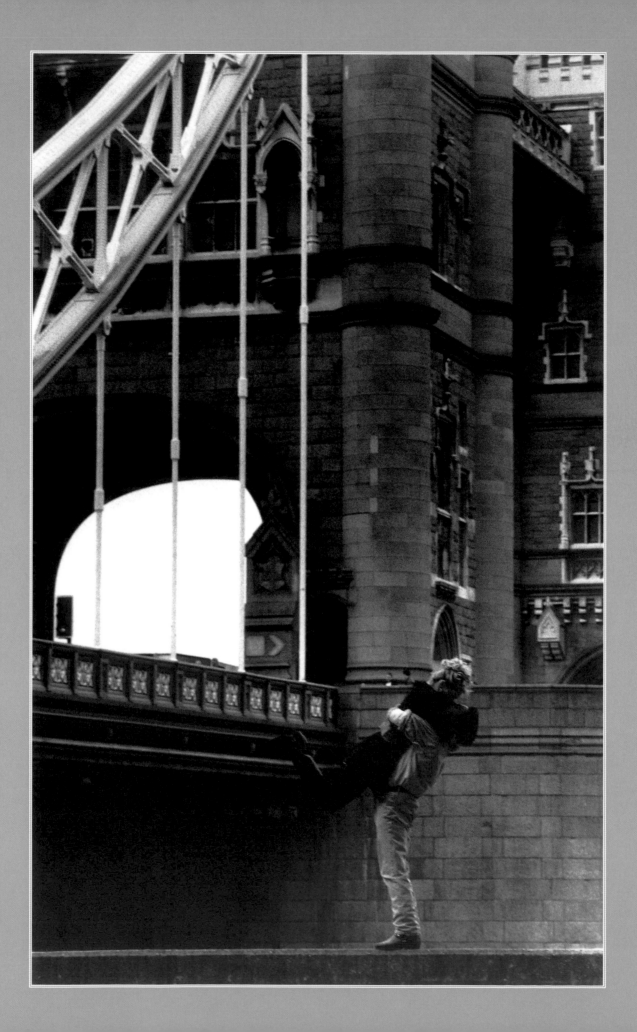

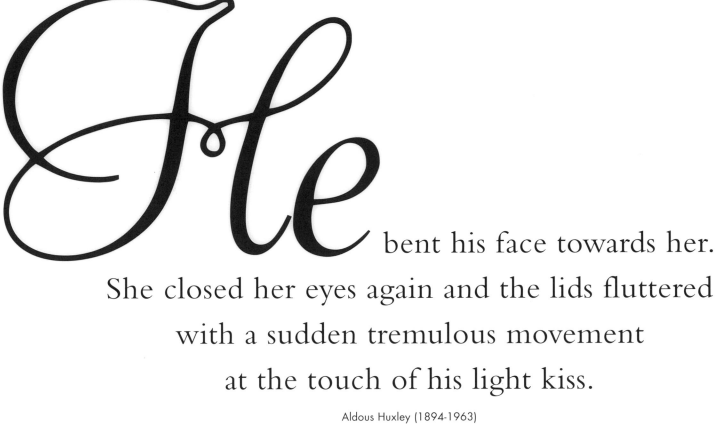

He bent his face towards her.
She closed her eyes again and the lids fluttered
with a sudden tremulous movement
at the touch of his light kiss.

Aldous Huxley (1894-1963)
English writer

Being kissed on the back of the knee

is a moth at the windowscreen.

Anne Sexton (1928-1974)
American poet

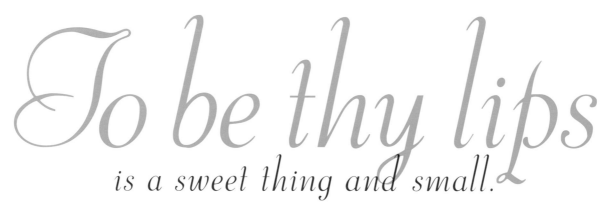

To be thy lips

is a sweet thing and small.

e.e. cummings (1894-1962)
American poet

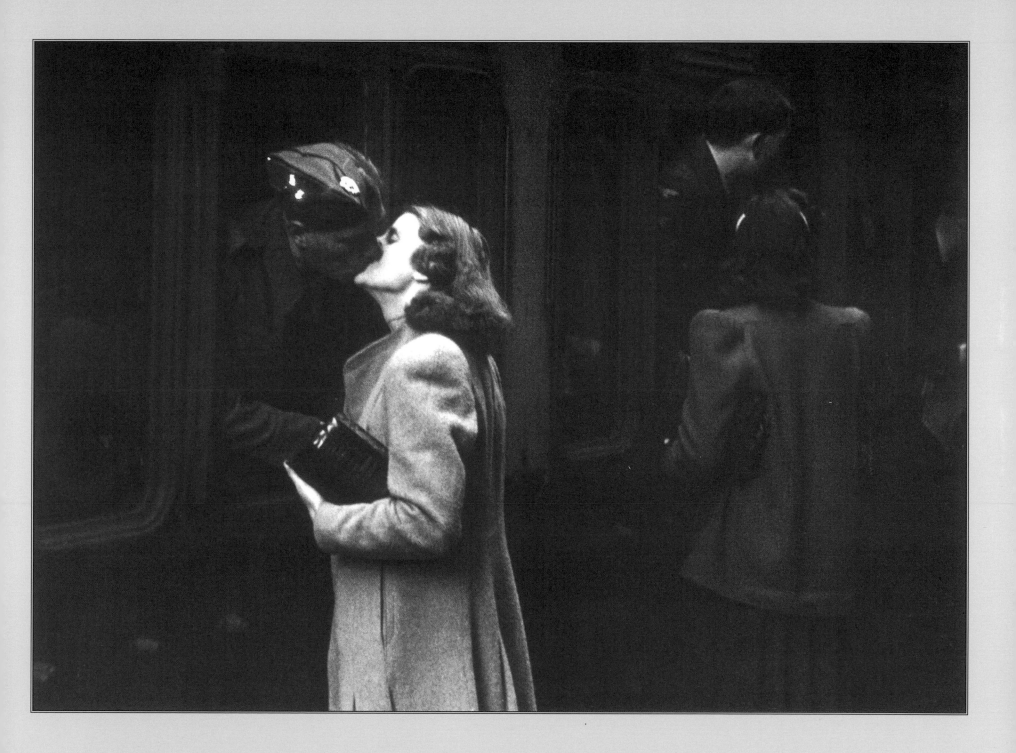

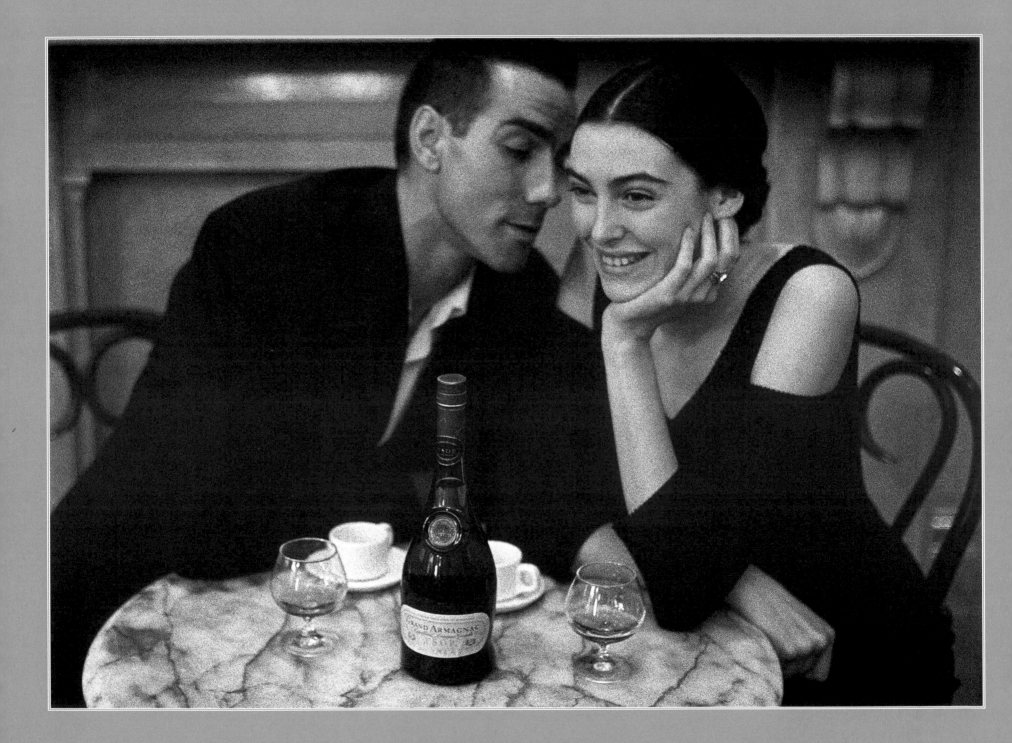

. . . how she felt when first he kissed her—like a tub of roses swimming in honey, cologne, nutmeg, and blackberries.

Samuel Sullivan Cox (1824-1889)
American writer and Congressman

Let him kiss me with the kisses of his mouth:
for thy love is better than wine . . .

Thy lips, O my spouse, drops as the honeycomb:
honey and mild are under thy tongue . . .

And the roof of thy mouth like the best wine for my beloved,
that goeth down sweetly, causing the lips of those
that are asleep to speak.

The Song of Solomon

I will leave thee when . . .
I have gently stolen from thy lips
Their yet untasted nectar, to allay
The raging of my thirst, e'en as the bee
Sips the fresh honey from thee.

From *Opening Bud* by Kalidasa
Fifth-century Indian dramatist and poet

Drink to me only with thine eyes,
 And I will pledge with mine;
Or leave a kiss but in the cup
 And I'll not look for wine.

Ben Jonson (1573-1637)
English dramatist and poet

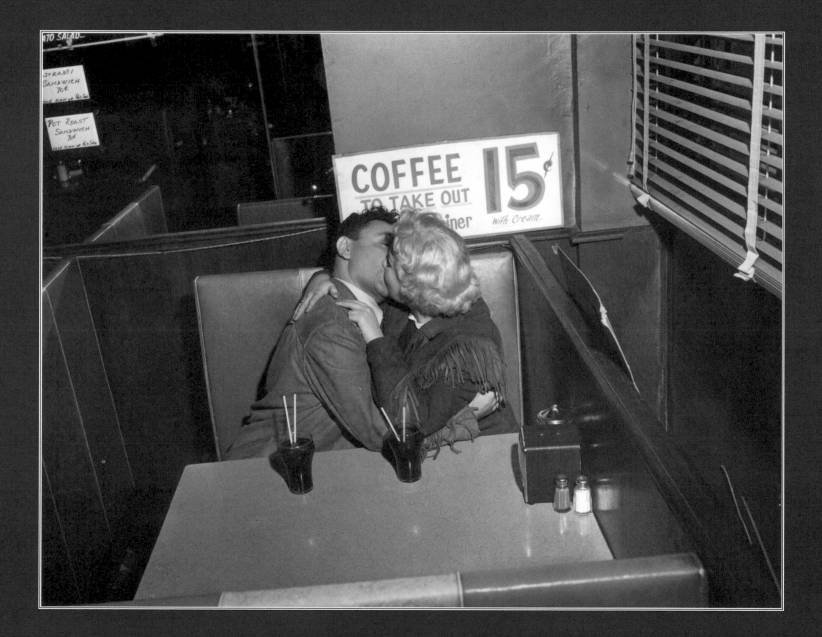

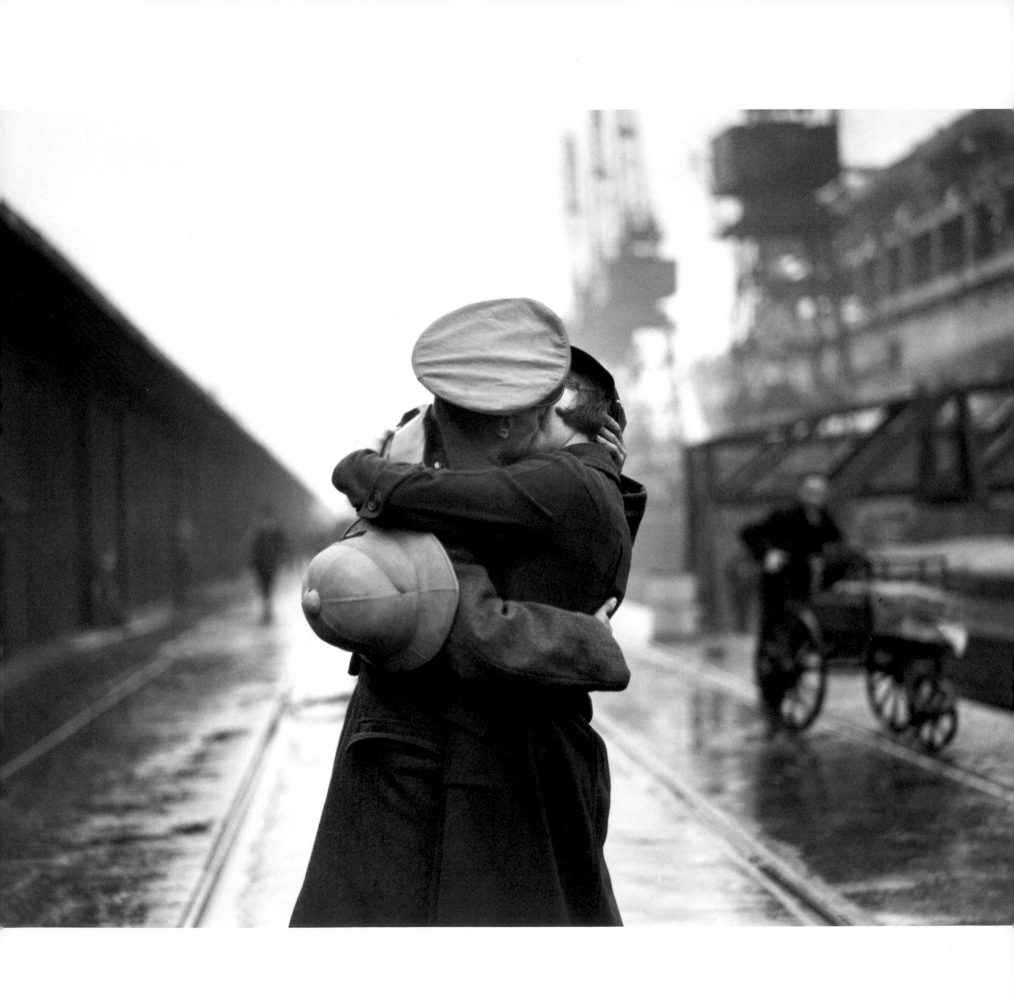

Consuming

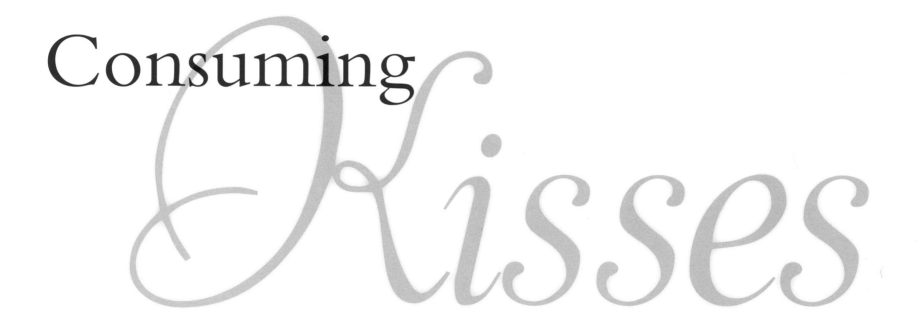

Kisses

Lips only sing when
they cannot kiss.

James Thomson (1834-1882)
British poet

The burned lip
will always spurn the flame.

Hugh Morris
20th-century American writer

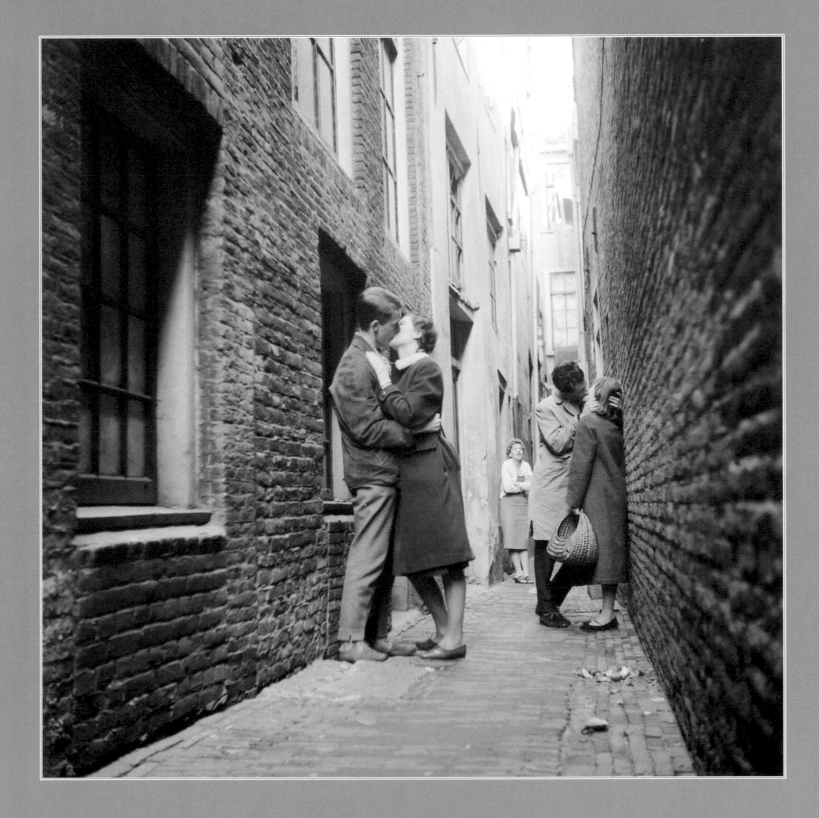

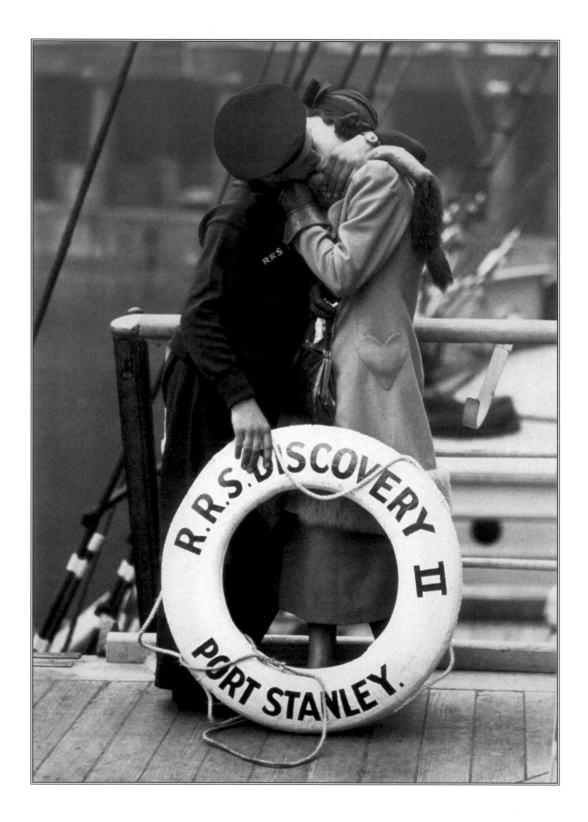

When I tried to draw near, you dissolved into air
before my lips could touch you.

George Sand (Amadine A.L. Dupin) (1804-1876)
French writer

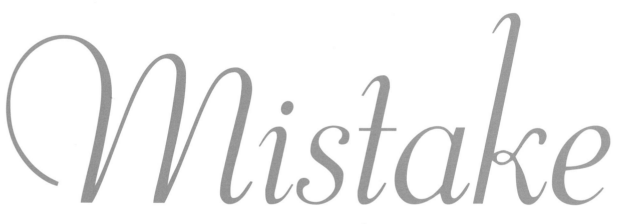

Mistake
me not—unto my inmost core
I do desire your kiss upon my mouth,
They have not craved a cup of water more
That bleach upon the deserts of the south . . .

Edna St. Vincent Millay (1892-1952)
American poet

The sunlight clasps the earth
And the moonbeams *kiss the sea:*
What are all those kissings worth
If thou kiss not me?

Percy Bysshe Shelley (1792-1822)
English poet

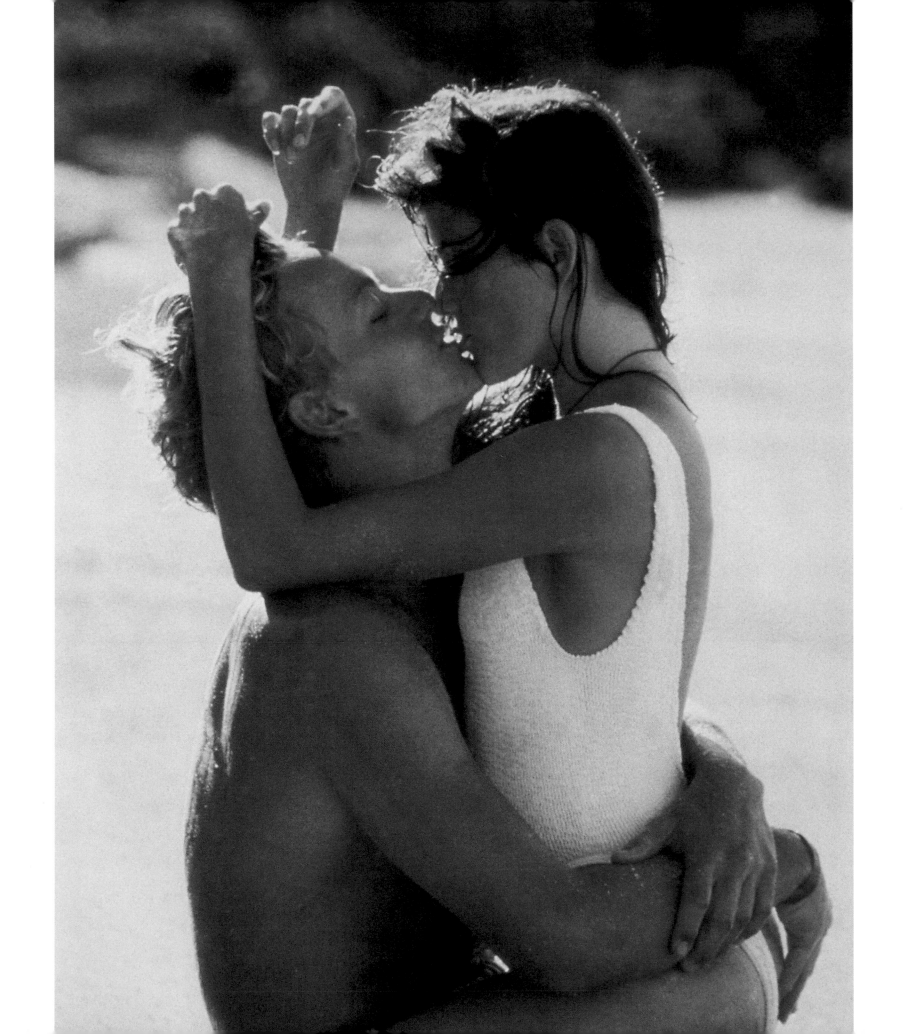

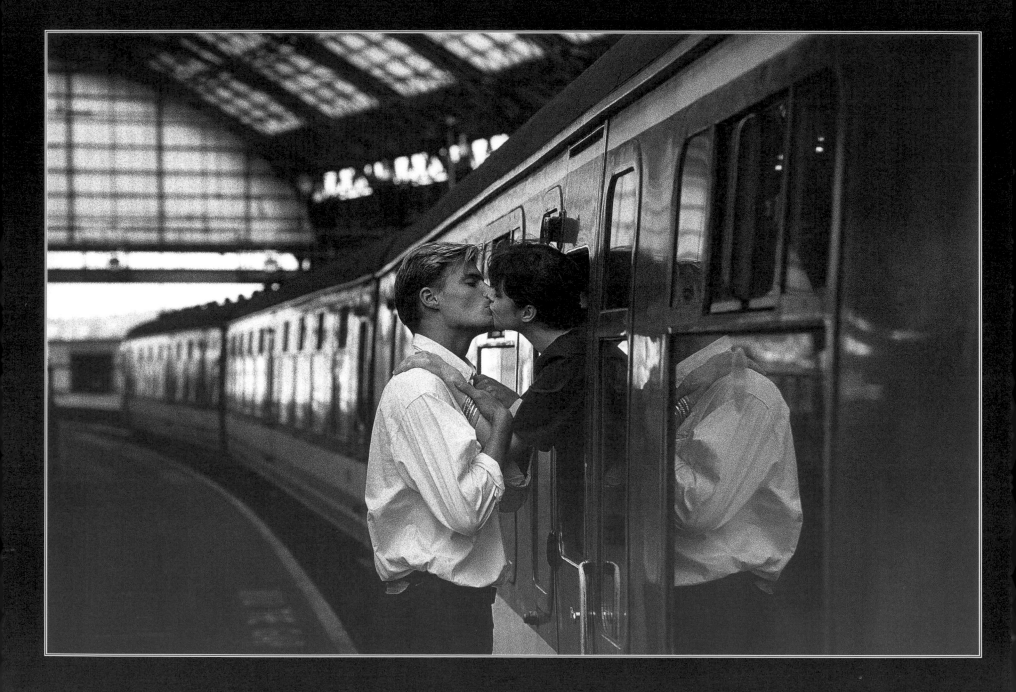

I cease not from desire
till my desire
Is satisfied; or let my mouth attain
My love's red mouth,
or let my soul
expire,
Sighed from those lips that
sought her lips
in vain …

Hafiz (1320-1391)
Persian poet

. . . is there still more in store for me when,
yielding to the profound feeling which overwhelm me,
I draw from your lips, from your heart,
a love which consumes me with fire?

Napoleon Bonaparte (1769-1821)
French Emperor

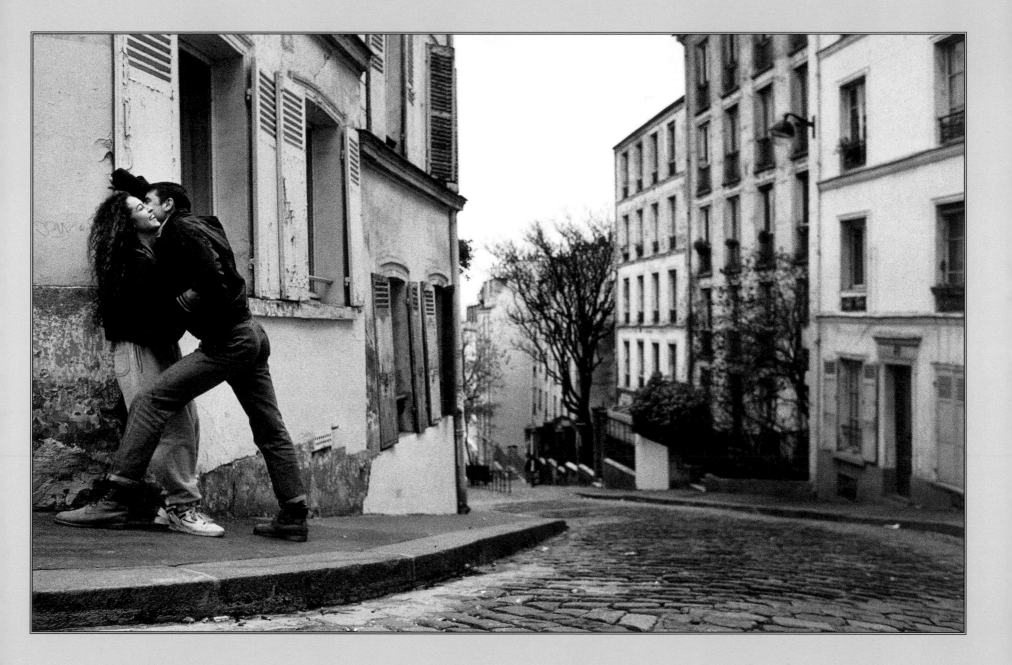

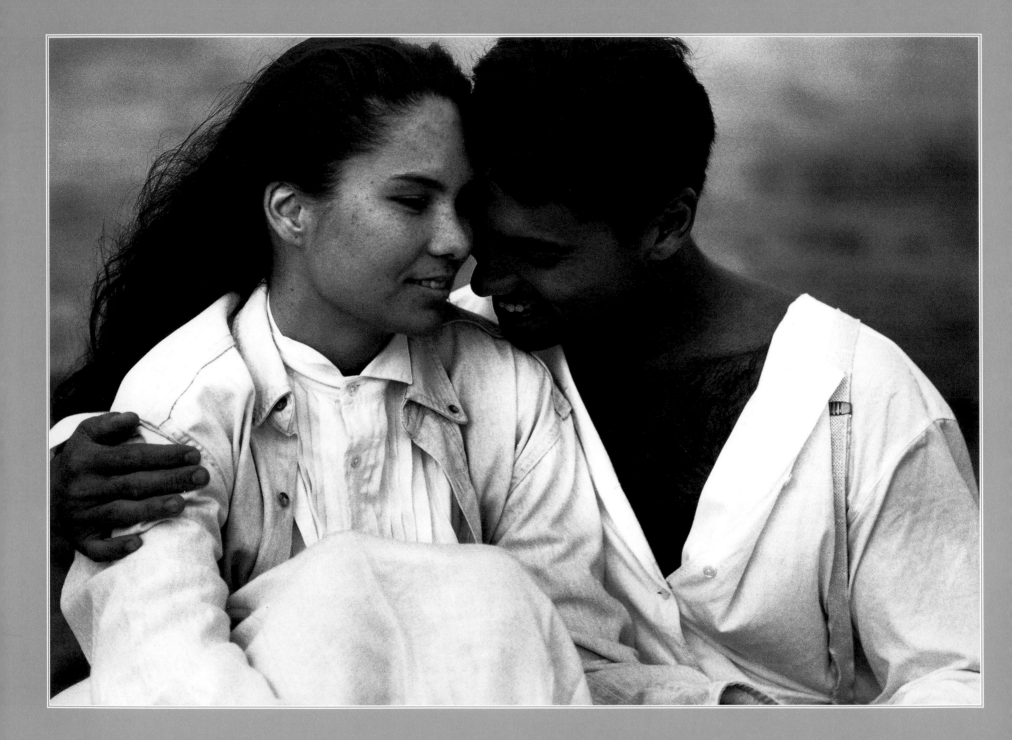

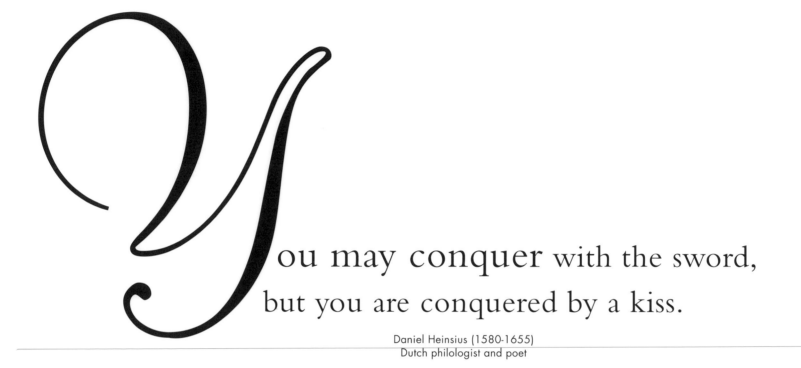

You may conquer with the sword,
but you are conquered by a kiss.

Daniel Heinsius (1580-1655)
Dutch philologist and poet

There are swords about me
to keep me safe:
They are the kisses of your lips.

Mary Carolyn Davies
20th-century American poet

A man had given all other bliss,
And all his worldly work for this,
To waste his whole heart in one kiss,
Upon her perfect lips.

Alfred, Lord Tennyson (1809-1892)
English poet

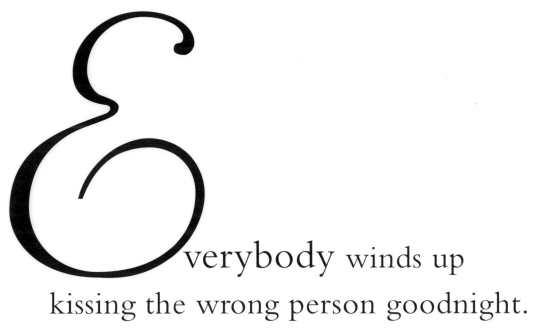

Everybody winds up
kissing the wrong person goodnight.

Andy Warhol (1927-1987)
American artist

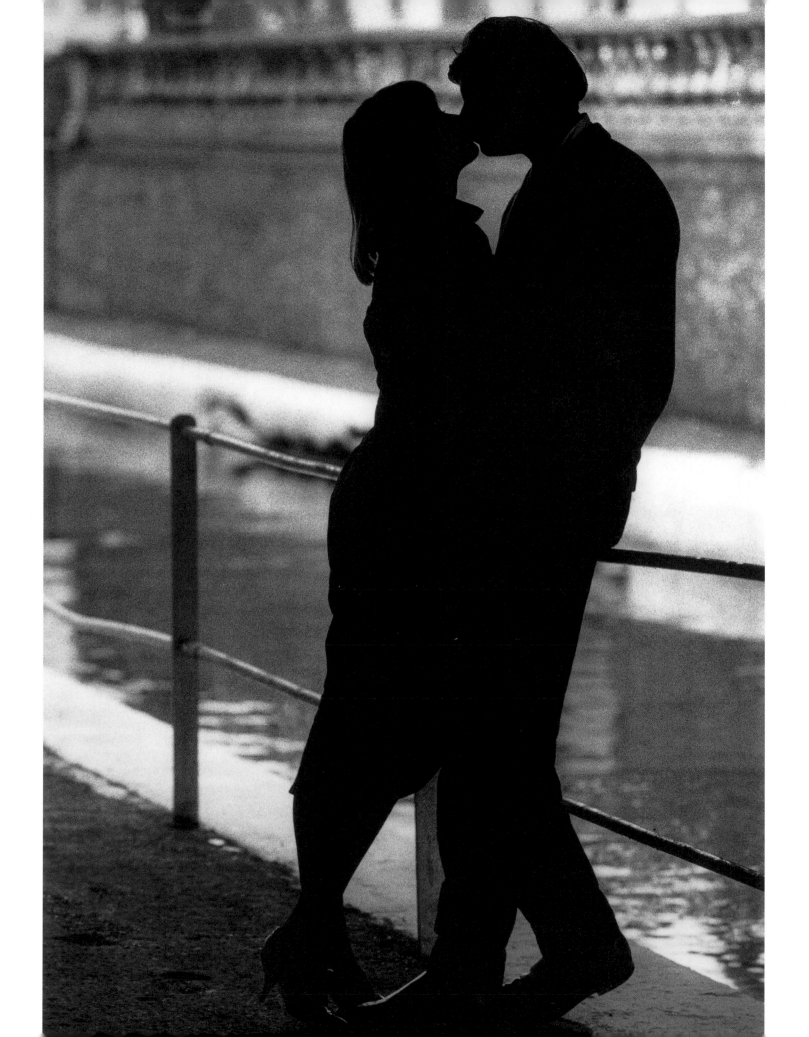

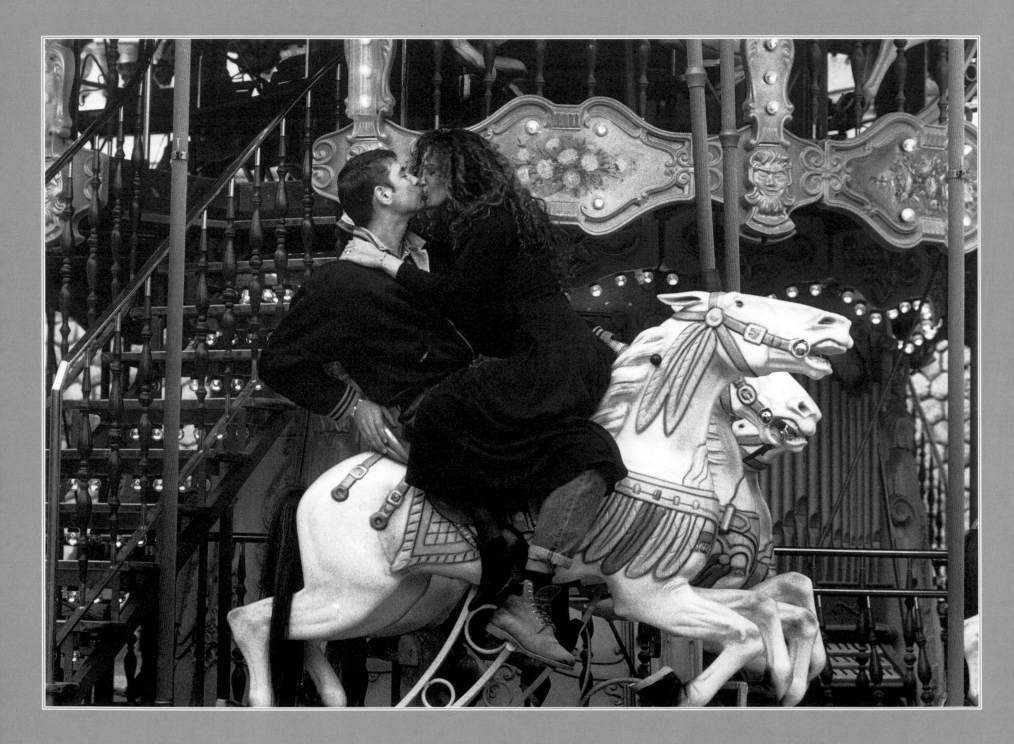

Cinderella, dressed in yellow,
Went upstairs to kiss her fellow.
But instead she kissed a snake—
How many doctors did it take?
One, two, three, four . . .

Traditional children's jump-rope rhyme

That farewell kiss which resembles greeting, that last glance of love which becomes the sharpest pang of sorrow.

George Eliot (Mary Ann Evans) (1819-1880)
English writer

"Then let us kiss once more,
as travellers setting out."

When she had done as he asked
and knew that her lips would not
touch his again and that
between them the recognitions of love
were ended, she felt him take
her hand and kiss it.
Then, knowing herself released,
she turned away . . .

Charles Morgan (1894-1958)
English novelist and critic

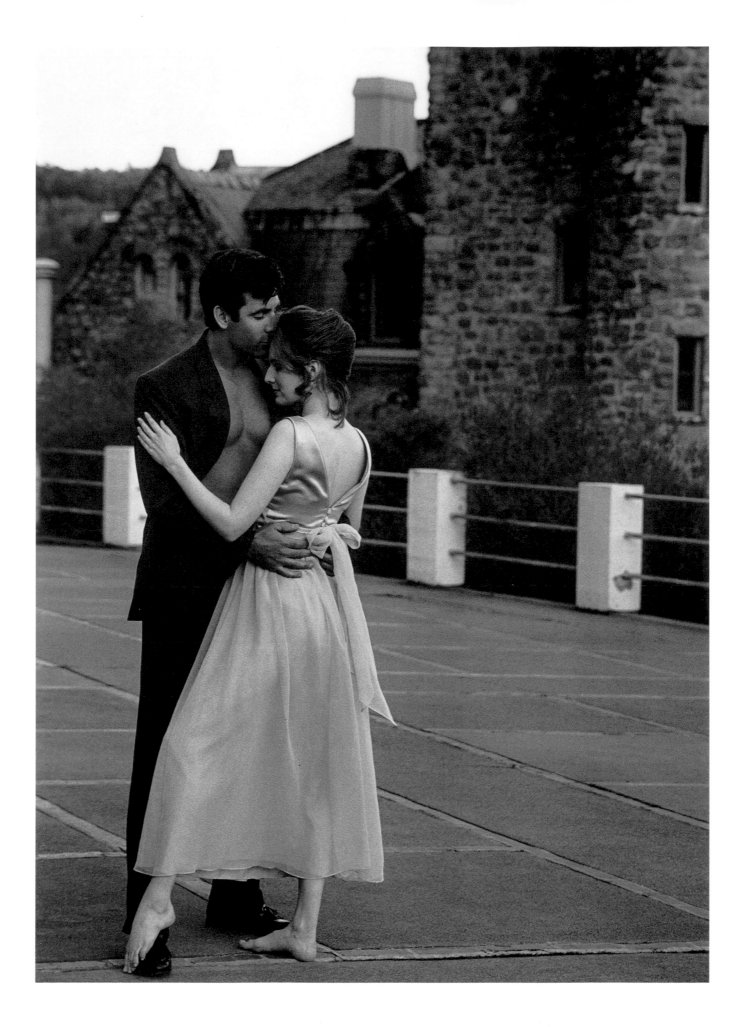

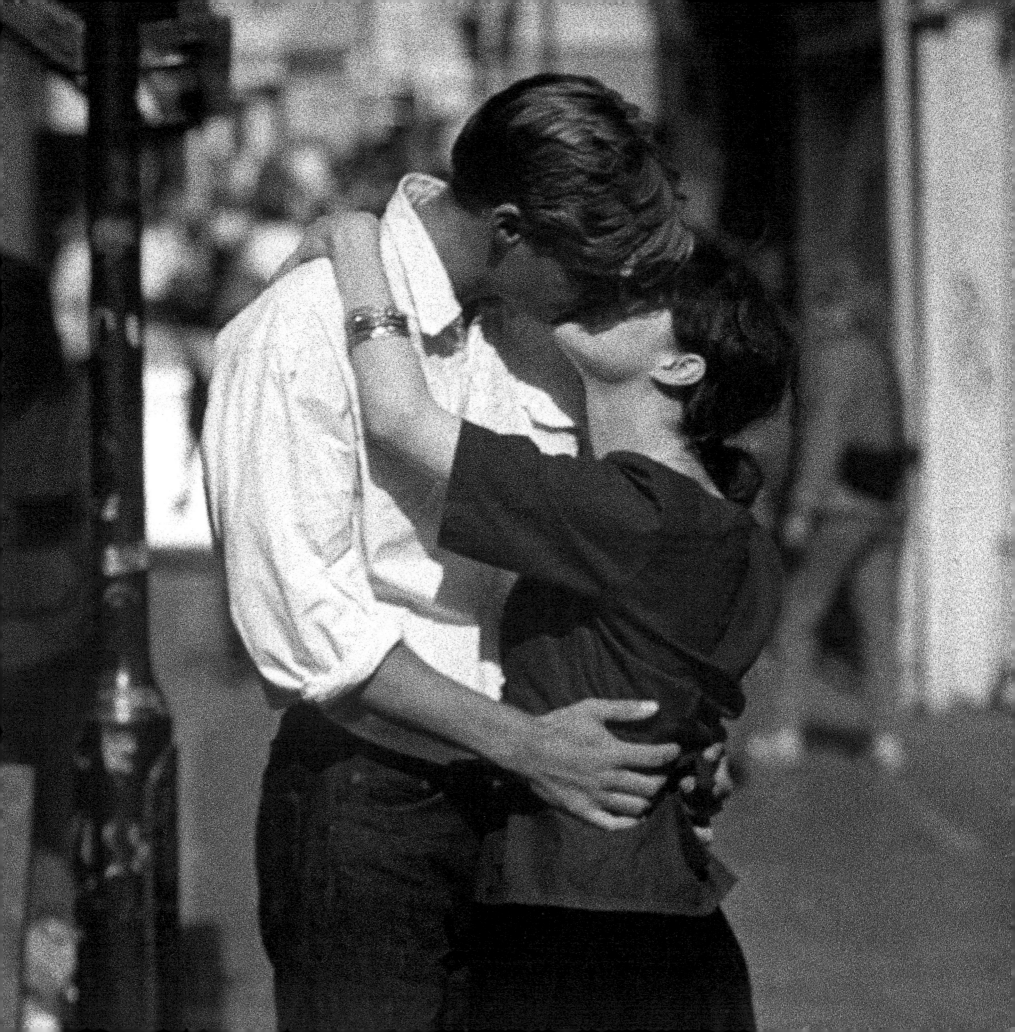

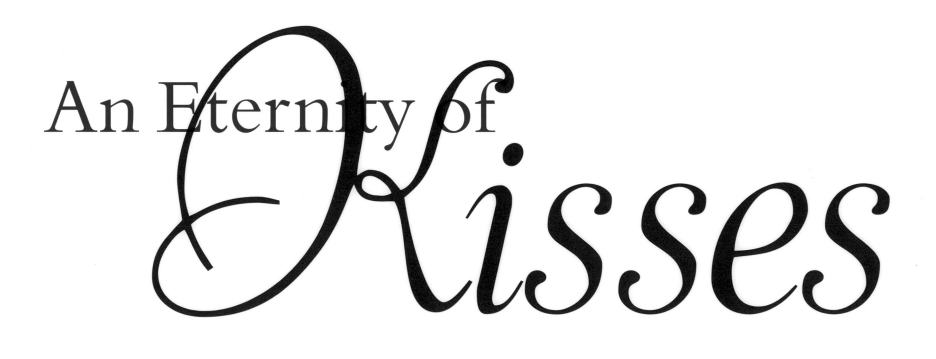

An Eternity of Kisses

. . . the kisses, which bring me back to life.

George Sand (Amandine A.L. Dupin) (1804-1876)
French writer

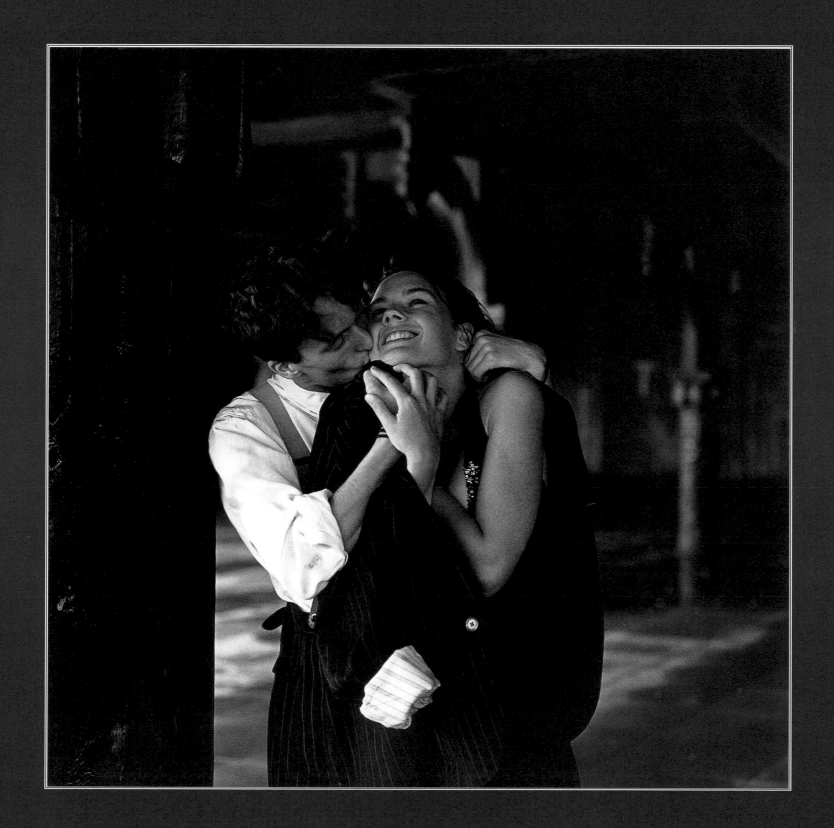

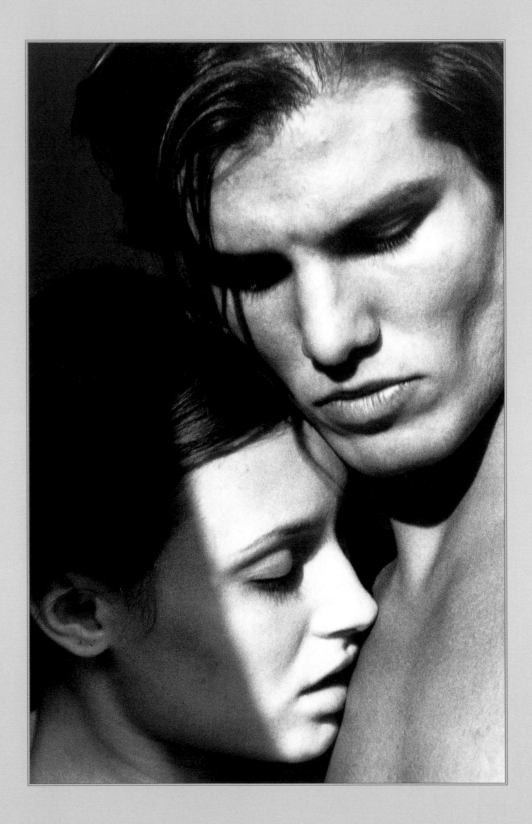

I dreamt my lady came and found me

dead,—

Strange dream, that gives a dead man

leave to think!—

And breathed such life with kisses in

my lips,

That I revived, and was an emperor.

William Shakespeare (1564-1616)
English dramatist and poet

There she lay, amidst the dust and the cobwebs looking so shining and beautiful and merry . . . that he knelt down beside her and gave her a kiss.

As soon as he touched her, the spell was broken; Briar Rose opened her eyes and looked wonderingly at him . . . they went down from the tower together, hand in hand.

Where one drop of blood drains a castle of life, so one kiss can bring it alive again.

The Sleeping Beauty by the Brothers Grimm, retold by Trina Schart Hyman
20th-century writer and illustrator

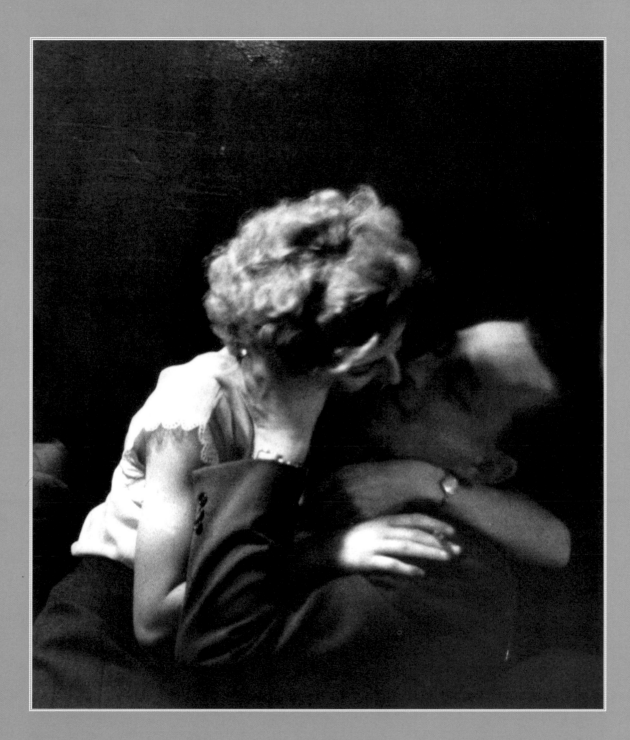

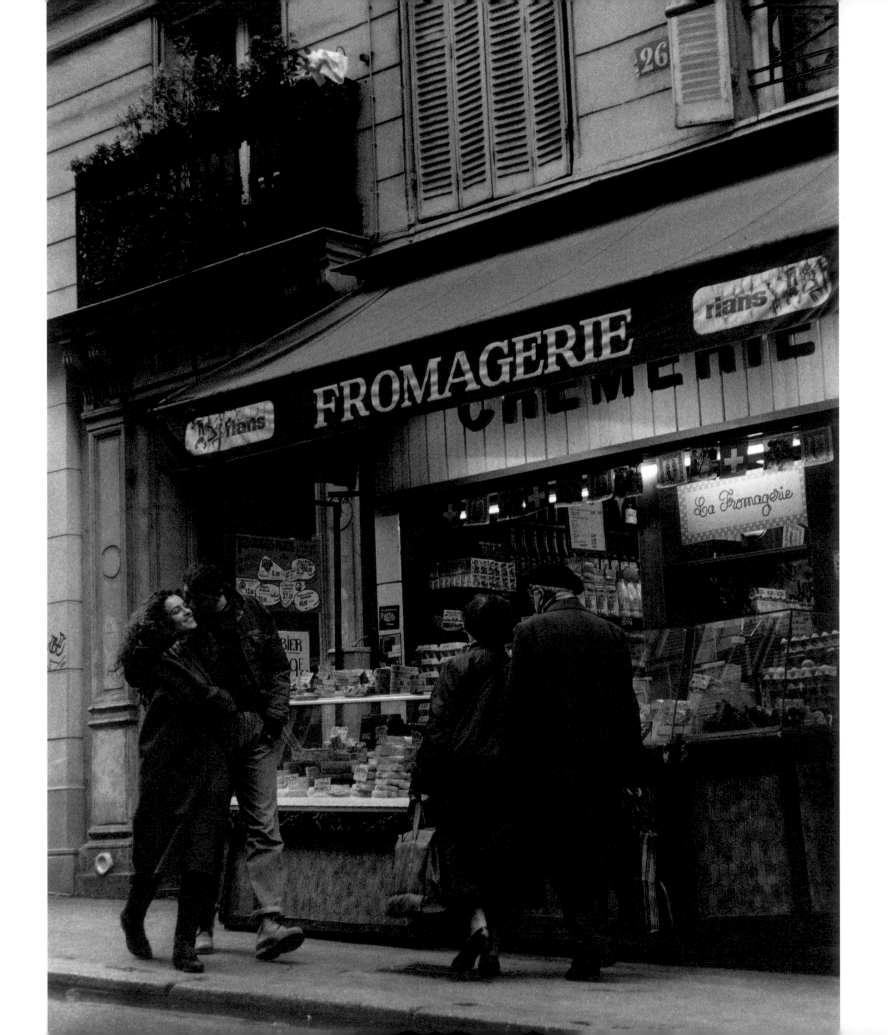

...*we kiss,*

and it feels like we have just shrugged off the world.

Jim Shanhin
20th-century American writer and editor

If I were what the words are,

And love were like the tune, With double sound and single

Delight our lips would mingle,

With kisses glad as birds are

That get sweet rain at noon ...

Alernon C. Swinburne (1837-1909)
English poet

Every kiss provokes another. Ah,
in those earliest days of love how naturally
the kisses spring to life! So closely,
in their profusion, do they crowd together
that lovers would find it as hard
to count the kisses exchanged in an hour
as to count the flowers in a
meadow in May.

Marcel Proust (1871-1922)
French writer

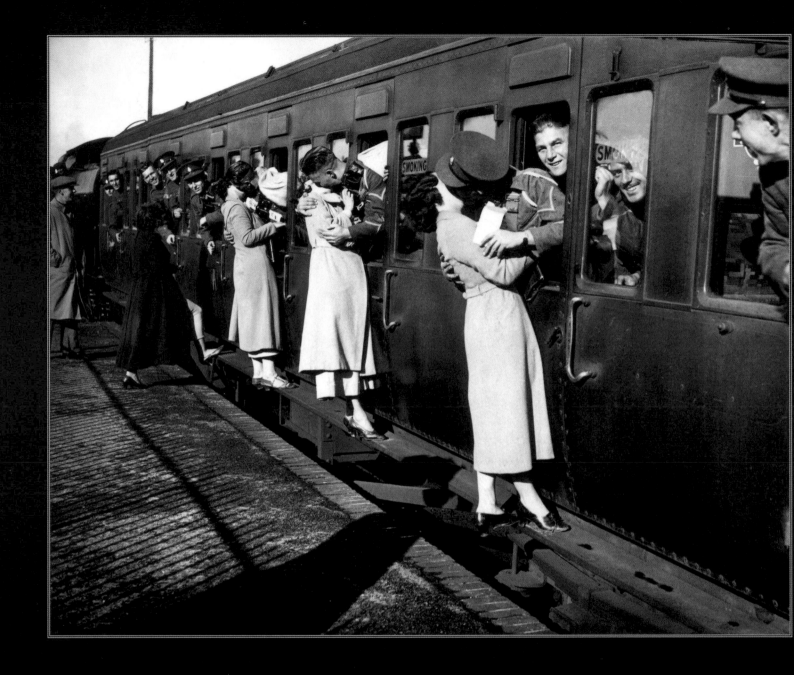

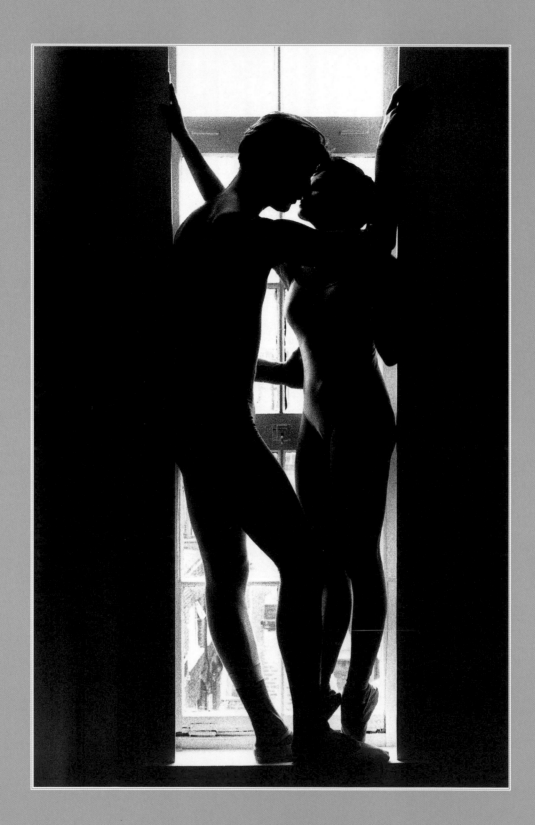

A thousand kisses
grant me sweet;

With a hundred these
complete;

Lip me a thousand more,
and then

Another hundred give again.

A thousand add
to these anon

A hundred more,
then hurry one

Kiss after kiss without
cessation

Until we lose
all calculation . . .

Catullus (84-54 B.C.)
Roman poet

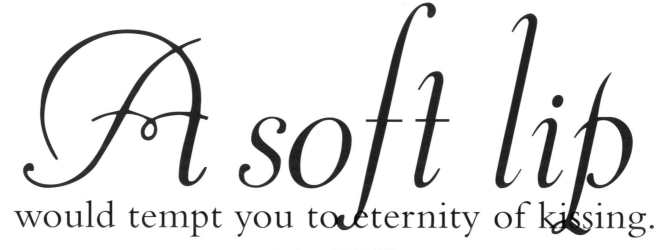

A soft lip would tempt you to eternity of kissing.

Ben Jonson (1573-1637)
English dramatist and poet

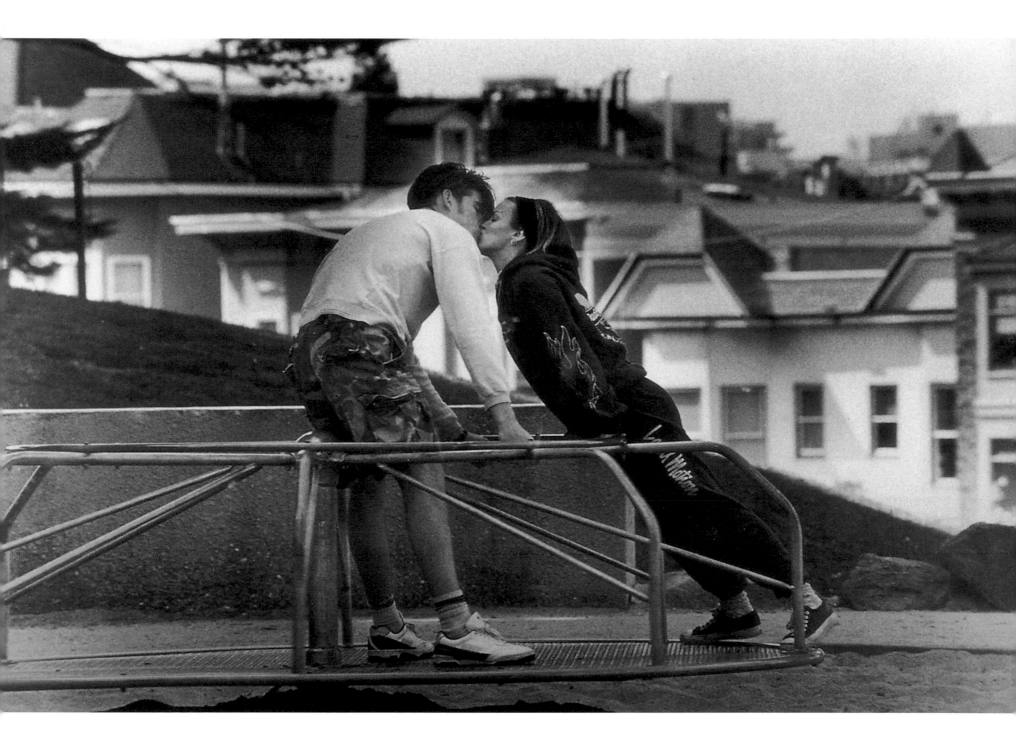

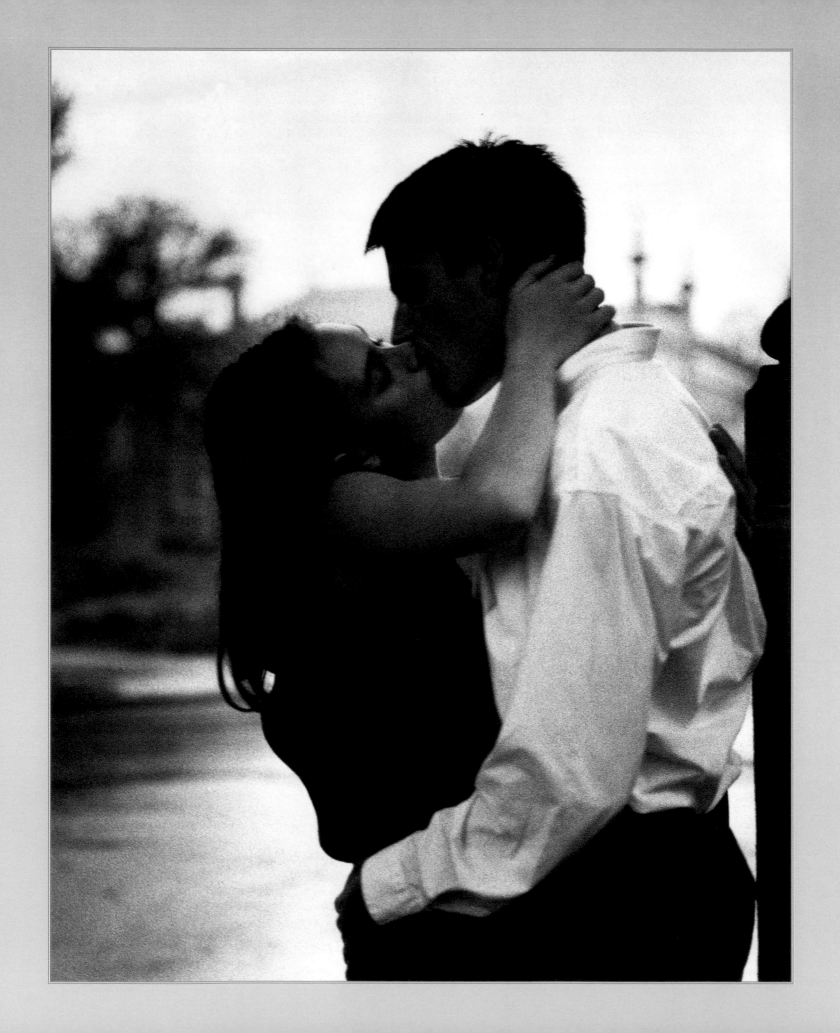

A long, long kiss,—a kiss of youth and love.

George Gordon, Lord Byron (1788-1824)
English poet

... *the promise* of such kisses ...

where would it carry us?... No-one could tell what lay beyond

the closed chapter of every kiss.

Lawrence Durrell (1912-1990)
English writer

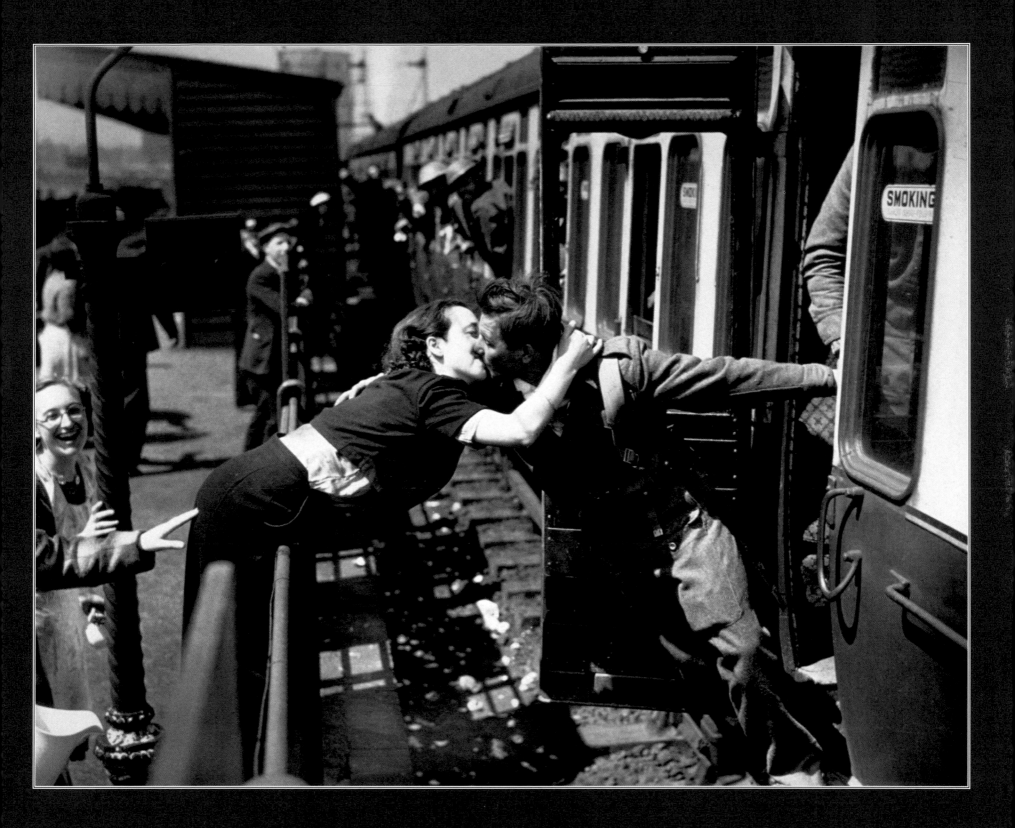

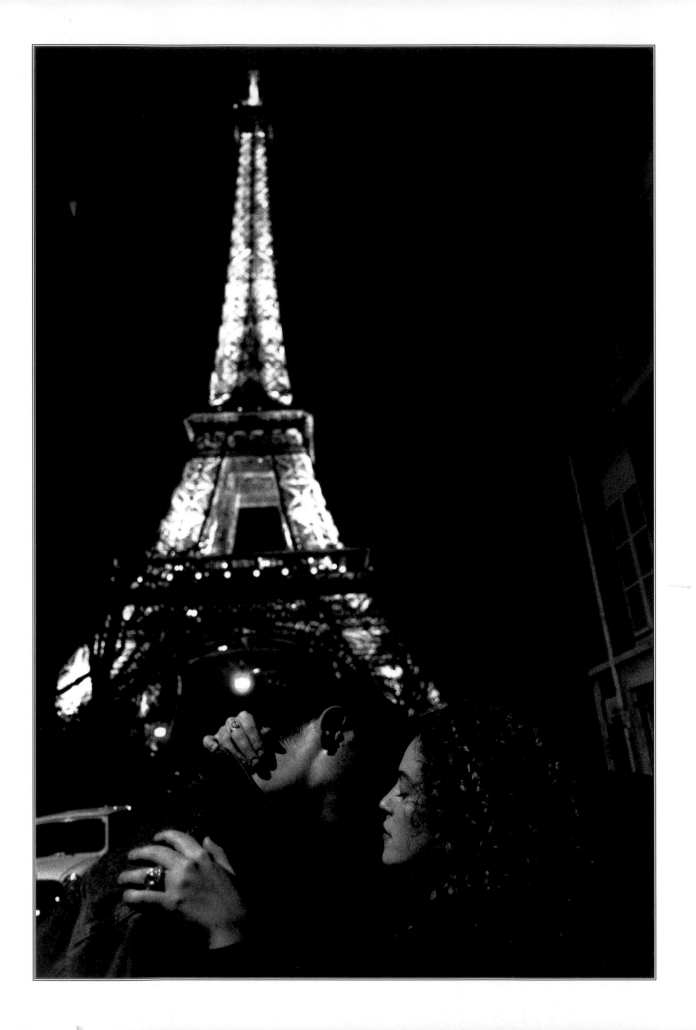

With a kiss

let us set out for an unknown world.

Alfred de Musset (1810-1857)
French poet

The universe hangs on a kiss,

exists in the hold of a kiss.

Zalman Shneor
19th-century Russian-Israeli poet

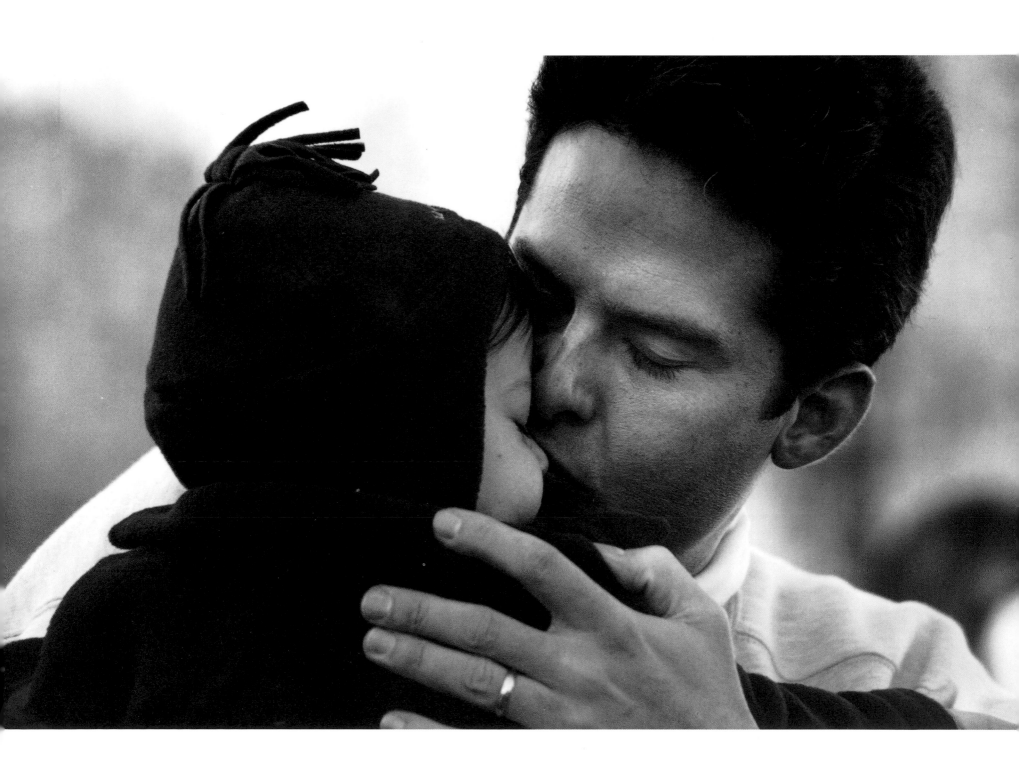

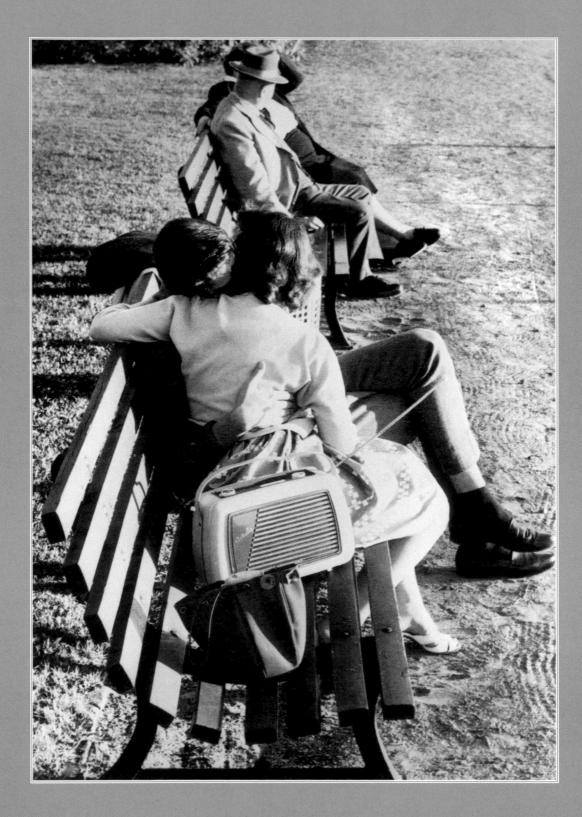

. . . then I did the simplest thing in the world.

I leaned down . . . and kissed him.

And the world cracked open.

Agnes de Mille (1905-1993)
American choreographer and dancer

credits